Incarcerated Lives Matter Movement:

The Hitachi Choparazzi Blueprint

By Hitachi Choparazzi

Dedication

This book is dedicated to George Floyd, Breonna Taylor, Ahmaud Arbery that sparked and ignited this huge scope for change in equality and non-stop spotlight on systemic racism. Also, Rayshard Brooks and my own Day One homeboy Albert "Twigg" Tucker from North Omaha Hilltop and Pleasantview projects. Along with an infinite amount of other Black men, women, and juveniles killed by the hands of police misconduct and brutality. May the Creator bless y'all souls in eternal peace. We are pushing for accountability and reform change so nobody dies in vain.

Also all victims of the 2020 COVID-19 pandemic that passed away and the survivors that made it thru these unprecedented times and adjusting to the new norms after losing their homes and jobs. My NYC cousins Derrick and Specc COVID passing.

Lastly, to lockdown society and Incarcerated Lives Matter. The movement and push for reform and to break the chains of injustice, inequality, and systemic racism in the criminal justice system. Also, to end massive incarceration with a united push as one. All the state, federal, women, and juvenile facilities woke and pushing for reform and self-transformation, and changing Black incarcerated narratives.

ATTN:

This work of art is from the author Hitachi Choparazzi's perspective, perception, and expression as an analysis. Partially his autobiography and life experiences as a Black man oppressed in the criminal justice system and lockdown society for years.

This non-fiction book is not meant to slander or demean people, entities, or organizations. This book is merely for the awareness to spread and a blueprint for ILM and society to follow to help change inequality and racism. Also to help lockdown society mass incarceration with their transition, self-awareness, life skills, and reentry transformation.

Lastly, a megaphone for the muffled voices that only echo inside a cage and have absolutely no means to be heard or resources. Also to show the flip side of the coin of police misconduct, systemic racism in the criminal justice system, and that Incarcerated Lives Matter, too.

Acknowledgements

Everyone that represents the struggle. All the victims of COVID-19 that passed away in the 2020 pandemic. Anyone suffering from inequality, oppression, and systemic racism. Lockdown society and Incarcerated Lives Matter Movement for reform push and following the blueprint. Finally, loved ones, influencers, and organizations who support ILM for the betterment and believer. Thx! My kids Kolany Jr., Pierre Keydale, Kylan, and beautiful, intelligent daughter China, A.K.A. Fine China.

God Mind Clothing and T-Shirt of the Week.us and Cuzo Byrd for helping make things possible on the outside. Along with ILM's other co-founder Brandon Hullaby.

Finally, my Omaha & NYC family, siblings, cousins, aunts, Mama Lisa, and sweetest lady on this Earth, my G-Ma Janie Lawson. God bless! Love y'all! Lastly, all the fans, supporters, urban shop owners with Billion Dollar Blueprint & ILM merch, and all my Chop-a-Style Publishing, LLC readers, thank you. I want to take time to acknowledge you all. Peace and blessings. Arabic salutations, As-salaamu-aleikum.

Contents

Prologue

Mid-November 2003

West Omaha, NE

Cousin Jackie's Spot, cold & gloomy

~ Flashback Suffering Experience ~

* * *

"C'mon, cuzzn, let's go bowling and get out of the spot for a minute... shit!" Cousin Jackie said sassy.

Choparazzi looked over at her from the couch and blew the sweet blunt smoke out of his nostrils like a Chicago Bull. He sucked his teeth, then glanced over at his Chopa-47 with a sly side eye, contemplating.

"Mann...Jackie, ya kno I'm on da run from the West Coast and got a damn warrant. I'm Gucci! Definitely not goin over north—and they just smoked twigg, too! Fuck da police—I ain't goin!" Hitachi Choparazzi spit venom.

Jackie put her hands on her hips and rolled her eyes as she flopped down on the couch, shaking her head and looking at Nae Nae's ass.

Nae Nae spun around on the couch and draped over Hitachi Choparazzi's shoulder and chest, rubbing it seductively.

"Yeah, Daddy, let's go and get out of the house..." Nae Nae said with a sweet tone, batting her eyes flirty.

"Mann...shut up! Nae, I told y'all I'm not goin nowhere, unless I got my rocket launcher with me...Fuck OPD!" Hitachi Choparazzi said sternly as he pushed Nae Nae back off him.

Hitachi Choparazzi's big homie C-Nut came up and slid Hitachi the blunt that he just lit up. C-Nut was over there with Jackie and for Jackie.

"Cuhz...let's go to Kelly's—Fuck it, Loc, feel me, hood?" C-Nut mumbled, high as an Elon Musk space rocket, scratching his chest.

"Fuck it, Cu...I'm hungry as fuck anyway. Y'all gangin up on a pimp! Nae, ya hungry, ma?" Hitachi lightened up as he pulled on the blunt and held it deep in passing it to Nae Nae gladly.

Hitachi started coughing consecutively, gasping as his lungs over-expanded with kush smoke.

"Hell yesss! Dammm it, Daddy...dat weed ain't goin nowhere— Breathe, niggah!" Nae Nae shouted as Hitachi waved her off. C-Nut passed him the bumpy face gin. Hitachi guzzled like a pirate. They all got up and left for Kelly's Bowling Alley over north.

Once they arrived at the bowling alley, Hitachi wasn't feeling it as he looked around, annoyed.

"Yo, dis some corny shit... Jackie, let me see ya keys so we can go get something to eat at Bill's BBQ. I wanna fuck up some ribs!" Hitachi Choparazzi smirked.

Jackie threw him the keys and Hitachi handed them to Nae Nae to drive. Nae Nae was from the West Coast, so she did not know her way around town. Bill's BBQ was deep into the north side off 24th Street and Ames Avenue. They pushed thru the north side, beating R&B chill music with a positive vibe.

Hitachi was killing the rest of the bumpy face gin bottle and quickly tucked it down on the passenger side, eyes lit like Lennox off of Belly, as he saw the cop car that sat awaiting at the light on the westbound lane off of 24th Street and Spaulding. Nae Nae just pulled up, awaiting for the same light on the eastbound lane opposite from the police car.

"Nae, hit your left blinker, babe... Bill's is coming up on the left. Relax, don't freak out, drive normal," Hitachi said in a low tone, barely moving his lips as he avoided direct eye contact with the police cruiser straight ahead.

"K-K, Daddy..." Nae Nae said nervously as she turnt left on green.

The police paused as he saw Nae Nae's blinker flicking to turn left. He hesitated, then drove straight thru Spaulding, continued westbound, then flipped a flagrant U-turn recklessly. Hitachi looked in the passenger side mirror and shook his head, regretting he left home without it.

"Nae, listen, they behind us. Don't panic. Follow my lead and turn off at Ames. Bust that right—fuck Bill's BBQ!" Hitachi said while still looking in the rear mirror and tucking the weed sack into Nae's panties, just in case. She turnt left; so did OPD, which confirmed they were definitely tailing her and picking them out, racially profiling. North Omaha is predominantly Black.

Nae Nae knew she didn't do nothing wrong or any traffic violations. This caused her paranoid senses to kick in, which caused her to turn into a dead-end industrial area. Of course the OPD turnt in right behind her and hit the cherry lights and blurped on her.

"Nae, listen, ma...we good. Relax, sweetheart. Cuzo Big Box gave me my New York cuzo's full name, Social, and D.O.B. to remember that's clean, just in case they swoop down. Once they run the name, we Gucci, babe..." Hitachi said unconvincingly as the two White officers closed in on each side of the car, guns drawn shoulder-length Academy style.

Officer 1 asked Nae Nae for license and registration. The second officer asked Hitachi Choparazzi for his I.D.

"What did I do wrong, Officer?" Nae Nae stated nervously.

"Why you want my I.D.? Am I under arrest or something?" Hitachi stated firmly with confidence accordingly.

The officer spit chewing tobacco at the car and shook his head, then told Nae Nae and Hitachi Choparazzi it doesn't matter. Nae gave them her driver's license, Jackie's car insurance and registration. Choparazzi complied too and provided them his bogus cousin alias. The police went to their squad car and came back within minutes later. They handed Nae Nae back her license.

"Sir, can you step out the car, please..." Officer 2 stated with a helluva demand outside of the passenger side.

Hitachi sensed and smelled the bullshit brewing with the dickhead cop. He sucked his teeth and sighed out angry and looked at Nae, shaking his head.

"Mannn...For what?! What did I do? Am I under arrest? See, y'all on some straight up bullshit!" Hitachi said, irate. He had that hostile fighter blood boiling, mixed with that bumpy face gin. He surely couldn't run, being boxed in. Then another OPD patrol car pulled up. The officer opened Hitachi's door and attempted to pull him out by the arm. Hitachi swiveled out of it and pushed the officer off of him.

"Damn it, I can get out—don't touch me again, cuhz! What did I do? I want a lawyer fa-real!" Hitachi stood up as he stepped out the car. The cop immediately attempted to put Hitachi in the rare naked chokehold snugged.

Nae Nae began to scream as Hitachi Choparazzi wrestled with him, which led to them tussling around the ground like wild gators, rolling hard. Officer 2 immediately placed his Glock hard pressed into Hitachi's back that Hitachi had kicked earlier. Nae Nae's screams became frantic and grew louder as she begged them not to shoot!

"P-Please, Officer, he just been drinking—Daddy, stop fighting. They gonna kill youuu!!" Nae screamed as the additional squad car jumped into the dogfight, rat-packing Hitachi. It looked more like a football doggy pile on the field. Nae was in shock, stunned.

One of the officers twisted Hitachi's arm while another one got a ground rear chokehold while resting his body weight over Hitachi's back. The officers were punching his face repeatedly.

"Fuck it! I can't breathe, muthafucka!! I can't breathe..you got me, fuck it! Bitch ass porky piggy!" Hitachi panted like a dehydrated dog having an asthma attack. Then he mustered up one last-ditch effort with all his higher power might and warrior spirit will to live, fight, and push them all up off him. He rose like an Egyptian king, tall up on his feet with the 240-lb. White cop still on his back attempting to choke him out. Hitachi was swinging wildly, but shortly dropped back down, winded, to his knees like a Spartan, and eventually back onto the ground. Hitachi felt his bladder release and a warm stream trickle down his leg, which he knew was a sign that his blood was trying to extract the rest of oxygen out of his body to his brain. More cruisers pulled up to the scene to join in. All punches and kicks went numb to the body.

All Hitachi Choparazzi remembered is dying mad as fuck without a real fighting chance, wishing he wouldn't have left the spot naked. Then he faded into the darkness and blacked out.

Nae Nae sat in the driver's seat, crying hard on the steering wheel, slobbering all on it with her seatbelt stretched and fastened. She looked up to see him lifeless, and the officers all circled around him as he lay still, handcuffed from behind.

"Oh my God—y'all not gonna get him help? Call the fucking ambulance! Y'all didn't have to do him like that either—fuck! Racist! Get him some help fa-real!" Nae Nae yelled, pressing the officers that were all looking dumbfounded until 6 of them picked Hitachi Choparazzi's limp body up to throw in the back of the cop car. Just as they passed Nae Nae in Jackie's car, Hitachi sprang to life!

"My heart still beating and I'm still breathing—bitch!! Fuck Officer Pratt! Rest in peace, Twigg, cuhzz! Rest in peace, Albert Tucker! Fuck Officer Pratt, Crip! Bitch, my heart still beating and I'm still breathing—fuck the law—y'all lucky I ain't bring my chop to air y'all ass out. I'ma shooter, baby. Rest in peace, Twigg. Project babyyy!" Hitachi Choparazzi spit in a tipsy rant, unfazed as Nae Nae lit up inside out and smiled.

She saw them lower Hitachi to hogtie him and fuck him up further out of the dash cam view. She even saw a blonde White lady cop punching him and spitting on him, too. Hitachi just carried on disrespecting the law, talking big boy shit. She smiled and knew he was fearless with big brave heart and they couldn't shut him up even after they threw him in the back seat of the squad car.

Hitachi had been shot before, a few rollover car wrecks, and a deep high tolerance for pain. Even though he had taken a beating for 15 minutes straight roughly, including getting choked out hard, he still didn't look bad or pumpkin-headed. He still looked handsome and bruised, not savagely bloody beaten. He always been a frontline pusher with a fighter spirit.

Nae blew Hitachi kisses and yelled, "I love ya, Daddy. We will be down there ASAP!" Nae screeched off.

The very next morning, Mama Lisa went downtown to Omaha PD headquarters, pushing a hard line and the issue to see her son Hitachi after the beaten brutality he sustained. He sat in the Bedrock small holding tanks. The problem is Bedrock did not allow visitors. It was just for holding and processing only. They told Mama Lisa he was waiting to be extradited back to AZ, where he had a Maricopa County warrant for weapon charges involving guns.

"Dega-Dega...you okay, son? Get up. Let me look at you," Mama Lisa said in a heavy New York City accent. Hitachi rolled over and opened his eyes, knowing only his Mama Lisa calls him by his baby name Dega. Also how Brooklyn Mamas are, you cannot deny them, they don't take no for an answer or bullshit, period. He stood up.

"My heart still beating and I'm still breathing, Mah. I'm good. How did you get in here, anyways?" Hitachi replied, sore as ever. That was the last time he saw his Mama Lisa.

Which that became Hitachi Choparazzi's mantra: "My heart still beating and I'm still breathing!"

* * *

Omaha, NE, birthplace of Malcolm X, home of billion-dollar guru Warren Buffett, Gabrielle Union, and home of the champ Terrance 'Bud' Crawford. Dating back to the Yellow Kid, Omaha has had its legends, but also has had systemic racism and inequality. Unrest from New York to Nebraska and globally. A push for social reform.

Foreword

What you just read in the previous prologue was an actual real-life experience and factual that was triggered from watching George Floyd's trauma being brutally choked out for over 8 whole minutes. Me and countless other Black men and women in lockdown society been victims of the same type of police misconduct and brutality multiple times and common situations. All that gets swept under the rug. I still wear my police brutality scars hidden under my tattoos on my face and arms that I try to forget about and refuse to look at or acknowledge because I still resent them officers and will not give it energy to curate and alter my mood in this already saturated toxic environment of incarceration and lockdown society conditions.

I am Hitachi Choparazzi, founder of ILM movement, currently incarcerated, locked down on a Level 5 supermax unit or SMU (Special Management Unit) in Florence, AZ. I am a general population inmate that has been in max custody hole for over 2 years now. Also suffering from an illegal sentence error, which I should have been home 2½ years ago. However, they refused to correct it.

I am a New York City native by the way of Omaha, NE, who currently resides in PHX, AZ, where I caught a state and federal case. I was the first Afro-American tattoo shop owner in AZ. Tattoo artist-turnt-author who wrote over 46 books, including movie scripts, kids' books, and tributes to Nipsey Hussle and Trayvon Martin. I created a library of self-development books mainly for ILM to help self-reform and transition with tools, skillsets, and self-awareness for successful reentry. I did a 180-degree straight turnaround with my life. I couldn't read or write until I got older. Now I registered my own Chop-a-Style Publishing Company, LLC, and literary agency, all from inside, to help us push and be heard, showcase talent, and freedom. Plus no traditional publisher or literary agency would respond or give me a real chance, being incarcerated.

They would see the letter from prison and throw it in the trash like we don't matter. Society, police, family, judges, institutions all make us feel like we don't matter or deserve to matter being incarcerated, exiled. No rights to live.

Therefore, I invite you and all friends to sit down with me and listen to my story, movement, push and see thru our lenses from ILM!

Bonus Page

I want to challenge you all incarcerated or in the free world to do a visual affirmation exercise in the mirror for 8 consecutive days. This is in honor of George Floyd over 8 whole minutes of being choked, suffocated, and saying he can't breathe.

Let's reverse this to create empowerment to push positive energy into the universe to all who read this book and create innate daily power. Your momentum will build and push forward.

This is how the challenge works. For 8 days in a row, when you first get up, go to the mirror and state your visual affirmations. State 3x:

"I AM LOVED"

"I MATTER"

"I AM POWER"

"I AM LIFE"

Then state what you are blessed and thankful for. Next, state what you want for your future or day. To plant the seed and speak it into existence.

If you miss a day, start all over. Have self-accountability and the energy to unlock your mind and push positive vibrations and seeds to grow in the universe. Thanks for your participation!

- Chapter 1 -

"ILM"

My heart still beating and I am still breathing! I am Hitachi Choparazzi, currently incarcerated, and I matter. Incarcerated Lives Matter, Black Lives Matter. For the longest, they made us feel like we don't matter.

This my platform I used to make incarcerated and Black lives believe and see they matter and to transition. I created a piece of art and awareness thru my work and leading by example of self-reform. Speaking from the heart and writing sincerely from the heart.

This book is not only just to open up dialogue or spread awareness. It is also to give a different narrative of mass incarceration and lockdown society. To tune your frequency perception and vibrations of lockdown society, the forgotten government slaves over 1.4 million Black men, women, and juveniles to modern institutions. Also to be impacted to take action or share this book, movement inside, and this blueprint creed to push for reform. If your takeaway from this incarcerated author's book is imperfection, it's okay, too.

I'm leading with my past failures and mistakes to relate and show if I can do it, then so can you by example. I've done everything in the streets you can think of: gangs, sold drugs, pimp, shooting, all the typical hood stuff no different from any other urban hoods city to city. Malcolm X did too before he reformed incarcerated.

However, I reversed this time and made it work for me versus against me. Did a 180degree turnaround with my life and used prison as a platform to reform, self-discipline, spirituality, self-awareness, and consciousness. Sometimes we have to go thru it to grow thru it. Regardless if you are incarcerated or not, it still applies. Elevation and education.

I love y'all. That's why I took the time out to handwrite a library, including this book, to help people know how to transition and self-awareness with love. To show all is possible. Just because you are locked doesn't mean you have to lock your mind. Rather, in quarantine or incarcerated, you use that time to unlock and tap into your mind. Learn self, know self, love self, appreciate self. The process of thinking versus feelings.

Reverend Warnock at Rayshard Brooks' funeral said God has a record using people with a record and named Jesus, Peter, and other prophets in the Bible. Therefore, he said you can't dismiss people with a record or incarcerated. I have a message and a voice to break through and connect. You cannot put me in a box, that's why I always thought outside the box and moved outside the box, formless like the air. You, too, can obtain mental elevation, inner peace, and sustainability. I'll show you how to connect and open your mind more in this book, too.

My push is also connectedness. The world is disconnected from incarcerated lives. Also, people incarcerated are disconnected, too, from their untapped true potential and innate self. We all obtain a superpower and strengths. However, you cannot play on them or discover if you do not know how or where to begin. Remember, if you don't know much, you can't do much! I extract value from prison to add value to you.

To the people reading this book or listening to the Audible and do not truly know all the hidden jewels, talents, and skillsets with untapped potential, I challenge y'all to tap in, see all these amazing people, and hear these extraordinary stories. Connect with them. To the people who have family, childhood friends, or acquaintances, tap in and reach out, communicate. This is the time to reach, teach, and amend while they are prone to listen and susceptible for change. Build connection proactively.

You can hear cries from the grave, but you cannot hear echoes of the voices in the cage? Interaction and engagement is key.

In order for me to enable you with my blueprint and ILM movement, I must tell you where I came from to understand where I've been and my art form of rising thru the oppression on the inside of lockdown society, and pressure against all odds is a real success story despite systemic racism.

This is my story rewind to forward. A snowball effect built into a tribe and movement with my signature style and mentorship, leadership, focus, and vision of innovation for all to push and break through!

This is my second time being incarcerated. I am known as a repeat offender with 4 strikes on my record of felonies, from drugs, robbery, weapons, and aggravated assaults with deadly weapons. Nothing I'm proud of or boast of, it's all part of my past and pain that I've evolved from. Just like the majority of Black men from inner cities, I was born in it and a product of my environment. Born into a vicious cycle of death or prison before the age of 25 that perpetuates like the four seasons.

Since birth in New York City, I always felt like I did not matter, especially since my family split and beef over my controversial birth. Being made fun of in the projects and at public schools from my family strife. I come from a dysfunctional background and broken family. I always felt like the black sheep of my family and the universal link. My family from BedStuy, Fulton Ave. My dad family from the Bronx and Brooklyn, too.

My mother and aunt both had a fallout of sleeping around with the same guy. Two sisters and one guy, that's how I was conceived with deceit and unintentional. My Mama Lisa was the younger sister who would go over to the older sister's house and ended up pregnant with me. My aunt already had been pregnant by the same man.

They tried to keep taking my mom to abortion clinics in the city from Staten Island to Queens. She would run out of the back doors of cars from my dad. She would fight with the family and half the family turnt their backs. Nobody did not want me born or to live with my scandal forever in their face. My Mama Lisa always said she knew I was destined to do something very special for the world. She seen and felt it.

I came out looking exactly like a light-skinned red version of my father. This caused my aunt and brothers and sisters that were technically my cousins, too, to be jealous and dislike me. I was the laughing end of every diss in the city. I guess that's why I learned to fight so heard. I would fight my half-siblings, classmates, and a horse if it would sneak diss me with that slick horse talk, too. This all made me tough as nails and developed a shell hard as a rock! Pretty soon those same jokes and slick heckles would bounce off as I deflected them the older I got. I developed hard calluses, like concrete push-ups.

I couldn't read or write because I did not see no real purpose at school. I'd rather hustle. School seemed fruitless and more of a fashion statement. We moved to Omaha, NE, because my GPa Lawson was a truck driver and found some cheaper cost of living areas. We went straight to the projects, of course.

During this time I had way more siblings, and my aunt and dad had way more kids, too. My dad was really absent in my life. I had my Uncle Dale and GPa Lawson, plus Quentin, who was my mom's boyfriend at that time that I thought was my real dad because I called him Dad.

I was the oldest boy on my mom's side. I had 2 older sisters. My brother on my dad's side was 5 months apart from me. One day I came home from school, got off the bus, and my Uncle Dale was awaiting to take us to the hospital for our little baby brother Peppy/Pierre. He had gotten into my mother's prenatal iron pills and overdosed. They tried to pump his stomach and flush it out of his system but it was too late. That next morning, he passed away.

I just remember seeing my Mama Lisa ride the hospital wall after the devastating news the doctor just crushed her with. I still to this day don't know how she made it to us and still could walk or a mother's pain, and I seen her whole spirit shift and broken. Still, she stood.

I was ten years old and couldn't believe it. Once I saw my little baby brother stretched out in the casket, I lost all my innocence and my protective warrior spirit kicked in. I couldn't even be one of the pallbearers and carry my little bro Peppy's casket. Couldn't process it all.

The next year my Uncle Dale passed away, too, of an aneurysm in the brain. He was 6'6" from Philly and would take me wrestling.

I couldn't cry at his military funeral because I was now coherent to death. Immune to the process.

Then my other father figure, Quentin, my mama shot at for breaking into the house. He ended up getting a lot of time for bank robbery, which all left me to the streets and typical hood stories. I was always a hustler from pumping gas, shoveling snow, you name it as a child and teen. I did it all. I took all my aggression out on the streets. We will save that for my autobiography, I'll go more in depth.

Fast-forward to my incarceration currently and what led up to it, then my rise from the inside and push.

My GPa Lawson came to see me in the Maricopa County Jail with my G-Ma Lawson. He told me if I lose trial and they could give me 12 years flat, I better sign the plea agreement deal for 5 to 6 years. I did 5 years flat and one month the first time. This is where I developed a new skillset and trade with the art of tattooing from the inside as a hustle.

Once I came home, I ditched the prior construction and craftsman trade to register and start my own tattoo business in AZ. Shortly after, I began to hustle again and working my Tropicanas in the strip clubs and avenues.

The feds were watching me, unbeknownst, waiting for me to slip to build a case. They had female federal agents stalking my house and me in the strip clubs. They heard I was involved in multiple shootings and had me further under their scope. I was oblivious the heat existed.

After a late desert night, I got into it with a guy play pimpin and I started popping Molly heavy, the only drugs I did in life beside smoking weed. I threatened him and told him I smell pussy. Next time I see him, I would fuck him! This was no doubt my mindset and vicious as ever back then, because I had homies dead or in jail for the life he portraying. I could not shoot his ass up then because the witnesses at the strip club and the cameras outside parking lot.

A month later I seen what I thought was his car outside of some condos and slept under it, waiting for him to jump in it or come out. However, the plot folded when a woman came to the car. Her eyes were big and she grabbed her chest. I apologized as I tucked the mini AK-47 in the side of my pants, dusted off, and skipped off.

Four months later I went to drop my strippers off at their apartment. I met up with one of my cuzos from the Midwest and we smoked outside, hotboxing in the Q45. All of a sudden, I see the guy and his car from the strip club that I had threatened prior. I had forgotten all about, but I knew I had to make good on my promise and deliver. It was about the principle.

I didn't have my gun on me, so I borrowed cuzo's .45, hopped out, and got live. I pistol-whipped him and stripped his ass down to his shoes and in front of his stripper broad, too. I caught myself just before I was about to pop him up. I was tripping and jumped in the car and sped off, which he borrowed a cell phone and called the law. I got into a high-speed chase and left the chopper and a few K-9 units, hopping in the yellow, lane going 100 mph to flee and cut off thru backstreets.

This was the first case I caught in the state after I got pointed out in the photo lineup months later. I thought I got away scot-free, but it came back to haunt me and my karma holding me accountable, SMFH.

My other case was federal, for conspiracy, drugs, and gun charges, then discharging a gun during a drug trafficking crime. Me and my cousin from Chicago that was living in PHX went down to Tucson to buy a hundred pounds to take to Chicago. However, my Tucson connect played middleman to some guys he got out of his sister's phone. Me and my cousin stopped at the strip club before going to the east side to one of my Tropicanas' spots.

Once they pulled up with the pounds, I went down to let them come in, and we weighed it and did the transaction. Me and my connect went to the car. He introduced us and as I was talking to the fat guy in the backseat, telling him it's all good and family to come up and let's go because we had a long 2-hour drive back to the far west side of PHX, the driver was fumbling under his seat and then stepped out and turned around while racking a .45 Colt in my face demanding me to give him the money. I seen my connect take off and scale a wall. Right there I knew I was set up. "Think quick, pimp!"

In my mind within fractions of a millisecond, I knew this guy had to be a rookie because back home, we don't slide the gun rack, we keep one in the head. It's street law. Milliseconds out here is the cause of life and death. No time for safety switches or to cock back! I was locked and loaded. I threw the half of stacks of money I had on me into his face and shuffled around the car.

I had my Gucci belt on a loophole extra tight. I usually didn't have it on, therefore made it harder to retrieve the 10mm Glock I had tucked in my waistline. I looked down at my chocolate Atlanta Retro Jordans and pulled with all my might.

I was timing him the whole time. He went to the trunk of the car to use as a shield and was raising to shoot. He was almost shoulder length. I knew here they come and quickly shifted southpaw my stance from when I used to box, figured I had less chance of that .45 hitting an organ and I'd still have a chance to shoot back. We were diagonal and 5 feet from the car yanking at each other. I am a veteran and been playing with guns since I was 12 years old. I tagged him first, then he fell on the hood of the car and hit me in the leg. We both dropped to the ground. I flipped my broken leg back around and emptied my whole clip. He never shot again. He only got a chance to get off 4 shots. Two people got shot that night and I was responsible.

"I got blood on my hands...I got blood on my shoes." —J. Cole

They went to the hospital different from mine and stuck to the street code of silence at first. Pima County Sheriff dropped the investigation without nobody cooperating. They labeled it a drug deal gone bad. I had a metal rod and screws in my femur bone from my hip to knee. They couldn't remove the bullet to this very day, labeling me a pimp with a limp for real.

I was out in Las Vegas for a while. The federal agents went snooping thru my trash on the side of my house and found Tucson Hospital discharge paperwork and went down to see why I got shot. It was a wrap! They got all those guys to turn state's evidence and flip feds testify against us. It's all public record. They told the other party that admitting to setting me up, robbing me, and shooting, that all they wanted was Chop-Chop—me.

I was facing 48 flat in Feds if I lost trial, which I pled out to lesser offense of interstate commerce, which I did not know what it meant. The state charges, I faced 28 years flat, too, and pled out to 10 to 12 years. Of course they gave me the 12. This is where my illegal sentence error came in at. They only charged us. I felt I don't matter again.

After the ATF raided my house, they found more guns, including in the truck I got pulled over in the day of the raid. I had charges on charges and knew I wasn't going to see daylight for a long-ass time.

My judge that sentenced me in the state ended up retiring. However, he allowed me to do all my time federal and ran it concurrent with my federal sentence.

Whereas, the federal judge that was a Black man named Collins sentenced me to 10 years and 30 months consecutively from my state sentence of 12 years. This is where the conflict and sentence error began. The Feds sent me back to AZ State. AZDOC refused to send me back to the feds BOP (Bureau of Prisons) because they were getting paid per year to house me and each inmate individually over 75k. The Feds told me the state of AZDOC had to bear the cost of incarceration if I got picked back up and extradited to the BOP.

This is why I have been stuck in limbo doing dead time. I lost appeals and lawsuits attempting to fight this illegal sentence error executed. I wrote letters, had emails and DMs sent out to different celebs, influencers, and organizations to help with my case and correct this unjust sentence error, which I once again felt like I didn't matter, was nameless and just an inmate number. My ego been humbled after I got sentenced.

The federal judge told me if I see a gun to run, else the next time I may not get another chance at freedom. Going to trial was like being dressed up in a suit and tie for your own funeral, getting buried alive. I couldn't see past that 42 years flat or let alone C-walk that 42 years down. That was triple life sentence to me. I couldn't use self-defense as a trial defense even though it was because I kept my mouth shut and did not admit at court or period that I shot back or shot 2 people attempting to rob me that night of the shootout. They stated all that. All I could do is sit back in a code oath of silence while I was about to get my back cracked without flinching. No bullets didn't humble or scare me being shot. However, being buried alive made my life flash before my eyes because I couldn't process all that time. This was the pivot of my transition phase to do a 180 turnaround. Then that same federal judge told me how intelligent I was but couldn't understand how I made such bad impulsive decisions. My state sentencing judge told me how intelligent and well-spoken I was, too. He said I handled my case pro se professionally. That I did more legal work, motions, stays, and appeals in a few years than most lawyers did in 5 to 10 years' time.

I represented myself because all my money, assets, property, and equity was gone thru resources for lawyers, private investigators, and my kids and family. I also didn't trust these sellout court-appointed lawyers with hundreds of other inmates in custody on their caseloads heavy. They didn't have my best interest at heart with my slew of charges.

My experience with being my own jailhouse lawyer was an innate process with transparency that allowed me to be an immaculate writer. From fighting for my life like never before, I've been a fighter with a warrior spirit no matter what I'm up against or the infinite odds and fatality. I don't see fear, I just see clear. Clarity, clear goals, mission, and accomplishing the dire task at hand. Besides, they say lawyers are the best writers, anyway. God was working me and preparing me with a new superpower skillset to enable me to write over 300 pre-trial motions, appeals, then almost 50 books to add a different element, perspective, and narrative to transition the world inside out.

Nine months after my incarceration, I was crushed by losing the last man and fatherly figure in my life...my G Pa Lawson. May God bless his soul. This caused me to further push and transition with my 180 self-reform to do something different, wake up and discover self. It helped me tap in further to my heart, mind, and spirit.

It was like looking under the hood of the car and you scratch your head, lost, not knowing what's wrong or where to start at. You wiggle the battery prongs, tap on the filter, and check your anti-freeze fluid levels. Then going to check and see if you get lucky and the car starts up magically. Next, you go back to lift the hood and this time, you see with transparency and with laser optimization exactly what's wrong and what to fix. Then, you start picking the engine apart with your bare hands as your tools. This is the power and energy shift I experienced after my GPa Lawson passed in the County Jail fighting my cases. They tried to slay me with a sword and gauntlet and I sidestepped it, stopping it with the power of my pen.

With my GPa passing, it left me king, the man of the family. I had no choice but to pick up the crown and take a seat on the throne to inherit my tribe and brace all my family with leadership, supportive roles, problem solving, emotional and financial support. I had to be the rock of the family and backbone. Even if I could only call audibles over the phones, so be it. I had respect and all the influence and power to move and shift my family forward to evolve in perpetual progress. It was just my presence missing and physical being. I just needed to get home soon as possible like GPa told me while he was still breathing.

However, I still had the queen and heart of my family, my dearest GMa Lawson. Therefore, I fought and went harder for my freedom. To this day, GMa Lawson is 83 years old, never missed a birthday, Father's Day, or holiday without sending me cards and blessing with prayers of love and positive energy. She always made me feel like I matter and never forgotten. Nor did she ever judge me or disown me from my past growing pain with the gangs. Whereas, my grandma in the Bronx on my father's side to this day shuns me away because she found out I shot some people and came back to prison again. I guess it's tough love. Really, I miss and love her, too, and needed her support and wisdom during this time and my transitional phases. It also can be my great-grandpa in NYC, her father, shot a police in the face dead and did all that time lost in the system, which I could have hit an emotional trigger to have her shut down from her prior experience. Either way, it's love and still my blood. I was just a product of my environment. No excuses.

Now that I was sentenced and hit the prison yard level 4 main line, I had time to reflect further. I shifted my focal points. My kids were split and torn. I had been married prior and divorced after my first prison bid. This time I've been married twice while incarcerated and divorced twice. My sisters laugh and don't take me serious because they say no matter how many ladies I move out to the desert, I will not find love in lockup, period. It's impossible because all women need physical affection. I guess I wear my heart on my sleeve because one marriage lasted 8 months and the other only 6 months. Of course it was infidelity or adultery which scar my heart further, but I took it as a learning experience and I looked at it as prison being a place and environment where you can't show no type of feelings or being emotional. Therefore, for companionship I was definitely blinded by my vulnerability. Those women also made me feel like I did not matter or incarcerated lives did not matter or have nothing coming. Being on the inside with lockdown society that was everybody's story, we did not have a worth, value, self-worth, and awareness or most definitely nothing coming.

Who made this mental block and damage narrative that dehumanizes all people incarcerated? The ones woke with hope or the ex-drug abuser and the ones with mental illness need not to be judged and guilty by a dehumanizing less than society.

This was another pivot turning point to trigger my transition for change and self-reform and prison reform grassroots planted. I started seeing a vision to reiterate the narrative and use a voice. Another vision to end mass incarceration and free the million Black men, women, and juveniles. A hundred years from now, they will be looking at mass incarceration to the equivalent of what slavery was on plantations in America. I said it first because I see it, believe it, and going to push a reform bill with you all united to change it. Amend the Constitution amendment.

Then I decided I can start writing my own books to be heard, build a platform for us to have a voice, and provide for my kids. I needed revenue and to get funded for my book visions and projects. Therefore, I had to work with whatever resource I got within my grasp. Starting from the bottom attempting to make something out of nothing was the easy part because I had been doing this my whole life. The only problem was that I wasn't in the projects, I was in prison. My "aha" moment was into a jailhouse hustle with commissary. I ran a store business 101 microbusiness entrepreneur. The trick was to scale and sustainability. In prison impossible is possible because when you don't matter at the bottom, the only way out is up, so I will take a billion shots just for one to make it out and enable me to get up. I started with this 2-for-1 concept, which works similar to a payday loan or check-cashing store. I give or lend them 1 candy bar, soda, ramen noodle soup, etc.; they'd give me 2 back, paying back the loan with interest. The catch was how to turn that into cash. If I could convert cold traffic from high-school telemarketing jobs as a teen, then I knew I could convert jailhouse commissary into cold hard cash. No doubt I was a brilliant thinker. Frontal lobe is the seat to my creativeness and genius. Also it was not illegal against the prison rules of conduct. It stated no gambling, trading, or extortion. It was no violations in lending, so I found a niche and broke through. Bingo! I can't get in trouble or risk losing all my accumulated commissary items from lender fees or tax.

First I went to all the heads of the cliques in jail, or what we call "cars," to sit down and lay out my business proposition of service. I explained to them that if anybody needed whole food boxes for the amount of $50, $100, or $200 in commissary in advance, I would lend it to them for a 2-week timeframe. In exchange, have their loved ones or girlfriends put that amount on my books/inmate trust account instead of theirs. Then, I pointed out the perks and it being beneficial with the instant demand and convenience. Mainly because once someone puts money on your books, you cannot get the store items instantly. It takes days later or even past a week to process, pick, and ship your commissary orders. Once it spread fast by everyone on the compound wanting food packages on the spot and became aware of the convenience, the supply and demand chain took off. My rates became the new norm. If I gave out $50 food boxes, I would get $75 back on my books. If I did $100, I'd get $150 back. And finally $200, I would get $300 back. It's all business economic development.

It was not easy at first because being in jail was just like the streets, same code. You did not trust nobody. The heads of the cars would look at me, trying to figure my motive because I was moving different and introducing something new to implement within. They wouldn't trust me fast talking, thinking I'm from New York City or looking at me like 'orange is the new pimp.' Even the guards would call me Pimpin because I was always hustling, working an angle, and all the pics I had up from my prior nightlife engagements with women. When really I wasn't pimpin, I was evolving and reinventing.

However, I used an experience I had found prior to the first time I came to prison doing tattoos. I had to reach out to the people, engage, and interact to get more clients and cash flow. Connecting to your community and creating great work and experience. I was branding with awareness and delivery, including customer service skills. This amplified my networking skills, too. Pretty soon bros came to me for legal work, divorces, child support deferrals, and the Muslim bros to do their name changes. I would get paid all in commissary and add it all into the pot of food boxes I was flipping.

I started seeing people follow my lead, listen to me, and seeking knowledge of how to do things. They obviously were all seeking change and were growing out of their pains, too. They needed correction and direction to enable them thru their own transitions. You can see all the woke ones, the weary, tired ones, and the Obama time for a change ones, I call them. Some sick of the street life, gangs, or drug abuse. Then I started thinking of a blueprint to formulate that they all can implement easy for change and self-reform with consciousness. The key was how do we break through to the masses and tap into that crowd. Of course I can go sit down with all the heads and politic, but the best way was course of actions. Any person on the yard, street, or life, period, you had to show us first, not tell us. You lead by your actions only. You got to show a Muslim something in the book and proof before you tell him to correct his action or if he doing something unorthodox. If you keep apologizing after slapping someone, eventually they will throw their guard up, counter it, and slap you back, or simply block. Your words don't override your actions. Therefore, I know I still have plenty of work to do and build a helluva foundation first to stand on before I spread the ism and jailhouse gospel reform and self-actualization wakeness.

Sometimes my energy and connectedness to the universe would be so strong, I still would have an innate smell of New York City rotten apple stench thru my senses that I would have flashbacks from those triggered senses. I would reminisce about traveling back in GPa Lawson's truck every summer to see my siblings, cousins, and grandma in the Bronx behind Yankee Stadium in Concourse Village. I would not see my dad as much, maybe one night at most. I felt like my grandma would push him to even do that. When I moved to AZ, I'd still go back to New York and Jersey to see my dad. As I became a man, I still never talked about my controversial birth, the strife and deceit or his absence in my life. I didn't seek his validation, I just wanted to feel like I mattered to him, which I realize after that last trip to Jersey, I didn't matter as much to him as he did to me, and that empty void grew deep and sank. Total disconnectedness. This is what helped rewire my brain to fire heartless impulses with no empathy or filter. It was like being on a journey soul-searching to find out your hero and ego are the same and superficial. Or your passionate project all your time, energy, money got washed down the drain. When life smacks you in the face, regardless of your age, it knocks the wind out of you, but you must not drop and fall. You got to bend with the wind formlessly and shift shape yourself back into form. Again, all these failures in this book and in my life is what helped mold and shape me to shift and spark this reform Incarcerated Lives Matter blueprint. Therefore, it's success in all our failures if you can down click it, salvage it, and learn how you failed, not to make the same mistake over and over again to root yourself in place or circles like an oak tree. If you water yourself, with time you can grow exponentially, like the bamboo tree. Imagine one man with the strength, structure, influence, and leadership skills to rise up to connect over 1.4 million Black incarcerated lives that they matter to reform and give them a blueprint to free themselves from all chains...mentally, spiritually, physically. To awaken the masses and equip them with a skillset for reentry is all possible. If only I can get up off the ground first to establish my independence while incarcerated, then to spread my campaign and success reform story I implemented.

Jail is the number one place for haters, too. Therefore this, plus my jailhouse lawyer legal writing skills, enabled me to be a prolific and elite writer with these books. Imagine having to write a book or something that everyone nods, gives two thumbs up, loves, or agrees on. To silence the haters on the inside is like trying to put a lid on the world and silence it, too. Someone always has something to say, whether slick, hating, or laughing sneak dissing. This is why jail I used as best feedback tools and get the best jailhouse book review. Really better than online Yelp or Amazon. It was all authentic, not fraud, plus people incarcerated had too much time on their hands and were brutally honest. They did not care or give a damn about your feelings.

Therefore, once I started pumping out books, I started with the urban novels, hood tales, which everyone loved, especially to hear about some pimpin because they were all curious and also wondered more about my story. Really, how did pimpin get locked up, which they all laughed at and shook their heads. By the way, I personally did not think nothing was funny about being locked up, I was serious. Plus they loved to get high and be around me or hit some laps around the penitentiary track with me, smiling and laughing at my life and street stories. It went into fictional book stories and they would read written page manuscripts in one day over 300 pages. They would want more and kept asking me when I was going to write a new one or sequels. I had the feds and state pen buzzing and my name ringing heavy. Then, someone asked me, "Pimpin, you gone type your books up?" Right there a thought bubble popped up!

First I wanted to get them on my education, personal development, how-to books. I would write different typesetting places to get quotes and samples. It cost around a thousand per typed handwritten manuscript. I still couldn't afford it with my microbusiness jailhouse commissary hustle. I needed help and to share my vision goals.

I wrote publishers and literary agents from the West Coast all the way to the U.K. to no avail. I got return-to-senders or letters simply tossed in the trash after seeing that Department of Corrections stamp and my DOC inmate number. I did not have or stand a chance without no referrals, even when I sent written samples of first chapters, prologues, and synopsis. They all made me feel like I, being incarcerated, didn't matter, too.

I finally mustered up enough money to get my first book, *Pimp of Da Ratchetts*, typeset and formatted PDF. I needed to find an urban book editor because I did not want traditional editors to look at my book objectively. I needed an editor with experience on urban novels. Especially in my Chop-A-Style lingo. For example, pimps don't talk proper or square. They wouldn't say, "Hey, I'm going to California." Hell no. They would say, "Say, P, I'm bout to shoot to Cali, baby." It's a difference and an essence to captivate authentic to make the novels more vivid that you can relate to or actually know someone's character like it. This was a superpower I tapped into naturally, therefore mastery seemed effortless. This is also when I started to realize the power of my pen and mastering words. Spoken words.

After my denials and turndowns, it pushed me to self-publish from the prison cell. The same concept as working from home, but in a cell. Nobody could see it or think it was possible. I decided I could find a print-on-demand company to print my books from one to a million all on demand. This would prevent me from having a cell full of books or my peoples' garages full of books, too.

My next step was to register my own publishing company and get my tax privilege business license and LLC from the inside. Another thing people doubted and hated on. I also had to get ISBN and STAN numbers and bar codes. My marketing plan was to sell to the prisons only because I can help and entertain them, plus that was my targeted audience that still bought and read traditional books. I designed my own brochures to print for facilities.

I started writing kids' books for other inmates' kids and their autobiographies, all for the low price of $50 on the inside. I know it's insanely low, but it's all facts. I got over the hump when people would tip me with a bonus that saw my shared vision and wanted to be a part of supporting something great. They would drop me $300 to $500 for a finished project and respect the hustle. By this time I would knock out full autobiographies or books in 3 to 4 weeks max. This helped me develop speed and delivery, which is how I was able to write almost 50 books non-stop.

With these funds I created my own publishing company called Chop-A-Style Publishing. Also created my own literary agency for incarcerated lives. I successfully registered and started them both from inside. I hung all my paperwork and certificates up on the cell walls to show incarcerated lives they matter and anything possible if you can see it and switch your paradigm, by reprogramming your subconscious to tap into your consciousness. Most don't know how to and are lost. This is my job to teach them and lead by example with my writing and building up by pushing thru all barriers. If I set the role right to follow my lead, the next man will go harder and adopt with his excellence.

Next I got another urban novel, titled *Hot Thots*, typeset and was going back and forth with the typist company when it got flagged by the prison and sent back to the typist after I already paid the thousand dollars for typesetting and PDF format. I found out that they had held a proof copy from *Pimp of Da Ratchetts* and AZDOC sicced a team of publication review lawyers on me and launched an investigation without my due process or consent. They blackballed all my Chop-A-Style Publications manuscripts, working with cover designers, typists, or publishers. Once they found out I owned everything myself from prison in shock, they told me I wiggled my toes under their nose. After banning me, my publication, and from any book practices, I appealed it in 30 days. It went as far as the AZ Governor Doug Ducey's office, which, after I stated my case and exercised my amendment rights for freedom of speech and creative writing, still upheld the state of AZDOC findings to ban my books. It all was a ploy to stop me from publishing. The main reason was suggestive language, content, and promoting sex and violence. I told them what book in the entire prison library is not? It's way more graphic novels and bloody than mine, no doubt. All factual.

The last ploy was I couldn't have a business bank account in jail or running a business. When really you can just by getting the AZDOC director of prison permission. Really, they wanted a tax and a piece of the sweet pie. Remember, the director gets a billion dollars per year for AZDOC money we never see. They cut meals, laundry, education, reentry programs.

The only thing I can do is write books and send them home. Once again I felt like they were all in cahoots and incarcerated lives didn't matter. I got shot down on my horse. I knew I would truly fly, I just had to tap into my infinite mind of will and ways, which I created another play. I went to building a blueprint brand that was based on Education, Elevation, and Innovation, which was a mentorship/entrepreneurship where we use those three core principles, EEI. I believe everyone has their own blueprint like everyone has their own unique thumbprint. It's my job to help you find it and tap into your discovery with my 3 core principles of Education, Elevation, and Innovation. Mine was the Billion Dollar Blueprint because I always had a brilliant mind, brilliant grind, and a billion hustles. I naturally had a direct insight and problem solving and a structural mind. I can look at the best in anything or any situation and make it a billion percent better. One day I was choppin and poppin with my cuzzo Byrd on the outside and he told me I did not have to stop hustling, I just simply had to switch my hustle! That clicked. I went on to push and print Billion Dollar Blueprint shirts, hoodies, and COVID-19 masks. Went viral in 6 different cities. I got into urban clothing stores on the outside from being incarcerated. All off cold calls on third-party three-ways. Some businesses I would flat-out say I'm incarcerated; some would appreciate my honesty and actually give me a chance and to get more exposure. This entire process gave me more push and enabled us incarcerated to display and break through with a voice and talent. We can still create a business, art, set up pay walls and market with excitement. All starting from nothing, extracting value from nothing in prison, using your time wisely and reversing it into a success story. A huge way to launch and it catch mainstream. Using the pen and being incarcerated for a launchpad of reform and creating or building life skills. Simply reinventing yourself for betterment inside these institutions as opportunity to build and create your own space. Remember, you got to see it to believe it. If I lead by example, that will make them relate from the same place and achieve it, too. I pray better than me, and they can pass on the blueprint decree for the next person and generation until we break through prison reform for mass incarceration.

I also got a home landing page set up for Billion Dollar Blueprint movement, selling my hoodies with a Teespring ecommerce affiliate marketing. I had my sister and New York, Omaha, Texas, Atlanta, AZ, K.C., and California family helping me push, purchase, and share online Facebook and Instagram with Billion Dollar Blueprint support for a real one and cause. They loved the brand, message, awareness, and movement. I listed the hoodies on my homepage website for $44. Then I would print from my cousin Byrd "T-shirt of the week" business and ship orders to different cities and states.

My next step was to add value and impact the youth, especially Black kids in urban cities. Therefore, I did modeling contracts, Billion Dollar Blueprint movement certificates. This was offered until they turnt 18. I would give them free merch every time I dropped a new style of merchandise in exchange for promo to referral my home webpage for billiondollarblueprintmovement.com thru word of mouth, at school, or public areas to promote. That was adding value, impact, doing good deeds, and good marketing.

I also used my website price point as a method of a practical tool to pry inside shops, meaning when I did cold calls and would get their company email addresses, I would pitch my price advantage point, telling them what I offer. I would say I sell online for $44. However, I'm offering you a wholesale deal for $25 apiece. They can sell retail $44 or whatever markup price they want for a profit. They can make a $5,

$10, $15 profit each unit of my merch sold. I would lay that out and get orders in advance, half or on consignment.

Once I got that brand off the ground, I had money to reinvest in my books and publishing company. I got my LLC and sold 500 hoodies online, went live and gave away a free hoodie to the winner of a raffle from my email list. Shout-out to Takiya! It was a process and a dream to get my LLC and register my publishing company with Bowker. Getting ISBNs under Chop-A-Style self-publishing LLC had people to finally see and believe. I started to help them with their blueprint discovery and self-reform transition.

I finally found an editor and a match to do all my books. I got *Pimp of Da Ratchetts* and *Hot Thots* fully edited and paid for successfully. I was able to push out *Pimp of Da Ratchetts* online, available at Amazon. Also created a Chop-A-Style LLC publishing page to be that dream library to all Incarcerated Lives Matter to help self-reform, transition, and personal development with reentry skillsets, from entertainment to screenplays and kids' books. Also to do deals with ILM to give them a voice and platform to be heard and display their talents and writing skills to monetize.

I have funding pages to help out on my book projects, all 46 of them, to self-publish and do Audibles. Also, IncarceratedLivesMatter.com to push our homepage with all events, newsletters, movements, and services for ILM. Everyone can tap in, whether incarcerated loved ones or not. I will be constantly updating it with my team support and, once I finally get released, for you all to follow.

Now my ultimate goal, besides self-reform from inside, was to be the first incarcerated author in the Library of Congress in Washington, D.C., which to be a published author inducted into the Library of Congress public record forever, you needed to have at least 3 books minimum published. This was a challenge after AZDOC banned me from writing books and publishing them while incarcerated. It was a personal goal because I couldn't read or write, and here I was, this icebreaker self-taught that wrote over 46 times what most people don't achieve a goal of one book in an entire lifetime. Plus I wanted to show my 3 sons to be better than me, and if I can set my mind to anything, so can they, all from tapping into their innate resources within to shine bright like a diamond. The highest vibration.

Now to share a story and a little history with you. They say if you want to hide something from a Negro, put it in a book, right? They want to keep us asleep while they eat, woke, building generational wealth, passing knowledge and skills down generations. The purpose of creating a library is for us all to read, educate, and seek personal development to grow. Keep us reading and conscious. Self-realization and connection.

It was forbidden since 1619 of slavery era in America for Negros to read or write. Some who got caught reading got lynched, mauled by dogs, or burnt alive with hot tar, pulled apart by two horses and thrown feathers on. It's graphic and heinous, but also facts. Therefore, hell yes, it's essential for me to read and write to educate all and push that our ancestors and forefathers that sought knowledge and attempted to read or got caught reading and writing did not die in vain or be forgotten for their great push that they paid the ultimate sacrifice before the slaves were free. Now you see my push for a Black incarcerated life that matters and incarcerated author self-published inside Library of Congress. The same place they store a copy of the Constitution that enslaved us, and still enslaves government slaves of mass incarceration that we need a united push to end. Hell yes, I do get a tearjerker sensitive writing about this, because I feel it and see things others cannot or feel. It's real and hit home to me because I was once out of focus until I unlocked my infinite power of vibrations and attractions to my frequency. I could have learnt how to read or write at school, but I was too prideful and had a New York City young boy ego early on. Hustle and trouble. Straight problematic.

Again, for you all that don't know about jail and what goes on in behind these walls and fences, it's no time for emotions in this concrete jungle where they prey on the weak and vulnerable. Masculinity and ego are the hardcore paradigms here. Therefore, when I lost multiple loved ones back home in New York City thru this COVID-19 crisis, I couldn't reflect out loud. I would go to the shower and shed tears to let the water wash them down and away. Plus I came out red-eye like it's from the hard jail water or soap got inside my eyes, irritating them, to play it off with my head up, chest poked out, march-stepping forward stomping the main line. This place is a whole different animal and can be lonely, distant, and dark. That's also why I choose to shed light to lead a way and clear path bright in the darkness. That they all incarcerated matter, not burden. Even if you a lifer or got double and triple digits.

My next inside endeavor as I would mentor people inside and help them with reentry, staying out with success and beautiful careers, schooling, and housing. All that implemented the blueprint reform stuck with it. Others followed the blueprint merely from seeing others' reentry success and the pictures and accolades. They were inspired and impacted then started to ask me to coach them and assist them how to do this or that and register their business or trademark their ideas, too. Right then and there, I knew I had a reform ILM Blueprint movement. I would do it to help, add value, and sole transition for others, not for money or to be seen. Only thing I want to be seen is my big heart. Only thing I want to show is all Incarcerated Lives Matter and have a chance to break through to better self, forget anything else. It's time to better you, for you, to save you. The first rule in life is self-preservation. It's law.

This working with people on the outside, including my little brother Poppy. I wrote 2 mixtapes and recorded on the phone he helped me produce. The others were from free beats I found. I wrote music for my P-R&B Album. P is not for Pimpin, it stands for Passionate R&B Album, because a lot of people don't know I got a passionate side to me. Passionate with my goals, visions, and work ethics including self-discipline. I love to say sweet things and talk all sweet into her ear day and night, especially in the morning or singing. The thing is, it's not for everyone's eardrums and private and exclusively for her. It's not dirty 25/8 like you think, either. It's just purely passion, confidence, and compliments, mixed with flirty silliness that intrigues the senses. Therefore, me to share that passionate side and songs I call it my passionate R&B projects, like that favorite lover track that got leaked on my page, too.

The Billion Dollar Blueprint track is dope. I did solo before Nipsey Hussle died in 2017 on my Facebook.

"Like Jay-Z & Nip...Hitachi got that Billion Dollar Blueprint... Education, Elevation, Innovation...They hating..."—Hitachi Choparazzi BDB—Hook, Animated

Next, my creative side on doing the urban novel *Hot Thots* soundtrack with the character from Atlanta, the M-Thot Sirachi, like the hot sauce bottle because he was hot in the ass, his song called "Tropicana." I brought it to real life how I articulated from the actual book. All the music vibes were all positive reaction and fed from the outside in.

Plus it also helped others see that they, too, can launch their music, EP, mixtapes, and write creative music, sounds, or treatment vibes.

My last successful project and challenge was making and designing my own brand of shoes, and I did it. Designed my own Red Bottom Urban Bugatti shoes. They were imported and foreign made in Italy by an Italian shoemaker with the fine Italian leather and suede. My goal was to give you that ultimate Bugatti style experience compact in the shoes on your feet. I even designed a special-made shoebox for each pair. The tongue is Burberry and the sole is red bottom puzzle pieces.

I started this invision on my Bugatti shoes two-and-a-half years prior before they came into finished product existence exactly how I thought, wrote, and designed it, including imported foreign elements. This proved more you can move in loopholes but you cannot get free from loopholes in the criminal justice system. My son told his classmate that his dad got his own Bugatti shoes and wore them to school. My youngest son said that people could not believe his dad did those shoes from incarcerated. Then my son told me they were alright for my first pair of shoes, the next will be better. I laughed. However, I knew my son was really speaking from the heart and saw the vision because I led by example for him to believe and knowing I would get better and better at it. They start to see and connect.

I would also have my sons go to take the Billion Dollar Blueprint merchandise into storefronts out there to deliver and pay them. I would teach them how to fold, tag, and bag them beforehand. Being a father behind bars is a challenge with being not physically present. Fathering over a phone, Facetime, and visit is tough and a balance you cannot master or get used to, including constantly providing support and revenue to let your kids see that they matter, too. Also your transition process and betterment kids need to see your sincerity, and that you love and value them to stay out and home in their lives always. All they need is your presence, not your presents. All kids want and need consistency with you men or women incarcerated, regardless of your troubled past or temporary incarceration. It's never too late to turn around and be proactive upon reentry in your kids' lives. Parenting skills.

My other big milestone great moment being incarcerated, pushing past oppressor barrier, was me being featured on a radio podcast interview special on Incarcerated Lives Matter and the Blueprint Movement, being the founders and the whole push. It was on the "Somewhere in the Middle" podcast, which I was able to call into thru jail. It was dope and a breakthrough for all us incarcerated. The whole prison yard was tapped in to hear me spit that reform and education transformationism and the blueprint. I actually end up getting 2 interviews a few years later after the initial one, thanks to referral of my talent, push, and ambition from the inside.

Let me share this old saying with you that people say, that jail is a step away from the grave. Even though people do get killed fresh out, I beg a difference. To us the dead get mucho (more) respect and they pain free. We, being incarcerated, have no respect or regard in society, underliers of that scum narrative that perpetuates on all of our psyche and permeates to the world, too. We are pushing to overcome that mass narrative. Jails are human dog-caged in rage, treated like a slave and filthy animal. It was originally for the people captured at war and in those concentration camps in Germany that the U.S. adopted. It was only meant as a temporary holding place, not life or decades and years on end.

I've currently been social distancing for 11½ years now. I recently been quarantined for 2 years now, too. Both being incarcerated and then segregated in the hole maximum lockdown because of my influence and push. It is a lot that goes on in between the scenes. This was just a glimpse into my background and the elements I face still incarcerated daily, fighting for freedom and to free mass incarceration. All thru my lenses, including hurdling over obstacles and whole world being against you narrative. This chapter was long for me to explain in a brief this whole incarcerated journey I've been on that made me see and played in my mental that I don't matter until I woke up to reprogram my own subconscious to grasp and walk a self-conscious that I matter and I am somebody. Even though the role society, judges, and systemic racism from the police arresting us to the criminal justice system home of mass incarceration. You matter, she matters, he matters, they matter, Incarcerated Lives Matter, Black Lives Matter!

Now that you've seen my character, you can see my growth to the present date. I love to share with you all to be the staple to learn from, especially the youth, including my extensive prison discipline record from assaults, knifes, phones, drugs, you name it, I did it all and overcame all the madness that all stemmed from being lost and trapped in a world of hate. It's past hurt, trauma, and pain we all suffer from and do not realize it, nor how to evolve from these types of environments from jails to the hoods. This is where we need help to connect. How can we if woke society excludes mass incarceration, which needs a spotlight?

The institution says I have 500 people in the system on lower level custody yards with money signs tatted on their face like Nipsey Hussle did. However, I am not no founder or gang leader. This is the power of a leader and influence. When you have inside impact and influence, they keep transferring you or moving you around to stop your movement.

Also they never seen structure or someone to organize chaos like I do, which they dilute and poison your message, trying to smut it up and stunt your growth, progress, and reform. They cannot understand how or why I move, especially writing all these books without no research or internet access. Pumping books out, preaching and pushing betterment, self-reform, and how to transition from within with little or no resources. They fear it because it's foreign and something they do not understand. When someone cannot grasp it or something, they automatically fill in the blanks with their own assumptions and narratives. They will automatically assume gangs, or criminal enterprise, when in actualization, I'm all legit regardless of my past Crip affiliations and projects I was raised in. That paradigm I was cultivated in, they frown upon it and forever try to keep you stuck or trapped in. People can shift, grow, and evolve as humans. They cannot believe one man with such power to create and lead with such connectedness. However, truly, it's nothing new. Malcolm X reformed and read while incarcerated, finding himself, true core, and his calling. Nelson Mandela in South Africa, Cape Town, was the originator of pushing for education in the prisons. He told them just because they are locked up did not mean they could not educate themselves, which, after 27 years, led to the freedom of him and political prisoners. Imagine that. We, too, can be united to push and reform to end mass incarceration.

I want to end this chapter by answering most of you guys on social media most asked questions about me, okay?

First question was where did I get my Hitachi Choparazzi name from and what's the meaning behind it? Okay, we don't name ourselves, nicknames are given to us. Hitachi Choparazzi is one of my many handles. My original nickname is Chopa, which is slang for AK47. They named me that after using them and playing with them in my hood life. They call me Chop-Chop for short. Hitachi is used in two ways, as a name and an action. Back in 400 A.D., the year of the samurai, Hitachi was a sword and of Japanese origin. It was the kensu and the katana sword era, too. Hitachi is also an expression used to chop something or someone getting cracked, like Hitachi off those animations from Japan. We use as slang, too. So anybody can get Hitachi'd anytime or a dice game, etc. It wasn't AKs then.

Choparazzi is what they started calling me in the inside as another handle. Choparazzi is synonymous to Chopa. When you shoot one, all you see is the flash and light up from the barrel muzzle flash, just like the paparazzi. And there you have it.

That mixtape track "Hitachi Choparazzi" featuring my little bro Poppy is catchy and also got leaked online. Poppy produced it and did an amazing dope freestyle for his verse. I know that one got thousands of views and downloads, too.

The next most asked question is what is Chop-A-Style? Chop-A-Style is my own personal unique niche style of writing and formulating. Also my publishing company and body piercing shop when I was home. The Chop-A-Style logo for Publishing LLC is the Hitachi sword chopping down thru books, mimicking the karate chop of bricks.

My unique developed signature Chop-A-Style of freestyle all my books just like JayZ straight from the head to pen, one-take jake. No rewrites, side notes, or exclusive intense internet research. Just a glimpse of my intellect, Gemini genius, and blueprint. A pick of my brain that I pride my style on that cannot be imitated. Also speed and time, the ability to write books in 3 to 4 weeks max. Most of all, my versatility to write at all levels and all genres of books, including writing screenplays. All self-taught with self-discipline, focus, and hard drive all wrapped into one self-imposed signature Chop-A-Style.

Finally, when do I get out, and what am I going to do once I get out? This question is from family and fans. Okay, I am suffering from an illegal sentence error being executed as ordered per judge. They have not corrected it. Therefore, I had to do an additional 30 months. My now projected release is late 2020 or early 2021 sometime.

My plan is to build more when I come home with my kids and relationships. My goal is absolute betterment. I want to push prison reform and to end mass incarceration. Do mentorships, life coaching, youth advocate, and speaking engagements. Finally, to build ILM movement to help incarcerated men and women authors get published. To teach them and to learn a skillset while incarcerated to have and continue to write once released. To transform effective writing skills into treatments, publishing articles, and content journalism, podcasts, etc. To be excellent and get creative writing skill jobs and careers. Help them transition and challenge themselves. To show them ILM and give them hope, awaken, and a future better. Most of all, to help with a successful reentry to their communities and to enable them to self-reform.

Thank you all for taking the time to read and hear my trials and tribulations, my injustices, and my impossible that did not break me, they help create and awake me. So many people dismiss your dreams, including loved ones, while you're incarcerated to make you feel hopeless, worthless, and impossible to matter. They will tell you that it sounds good waiting until you get out, or they don't know about that, we will see when you get out. I say, why wait till you get out, or wait, period? Start right now from inside. Use this time like I did to lead by example and reverse it! Make time work for you versus against you. It's universal law 101. Then you can reverse these narratives, you, and build self. I reached out to celebs, orgs, still no help or bailouts to save me. I kept writing, pushing, reforming self!

Chop-A-Style Publishing LLC

2020 Catalog

All exclusively written by Hitachi Choparazzi

Urban Novels

Hot Thots

Liqz

She Go

Reality Show 3D-HD

Pimp of Da Ratchetts

PODR II Vegas

PODR 3 Orange is the New Pimp

Bugatti Boys

Real Hot Wives of Atlanta

The Prosecutor

Big Pep & Plucker Story

Hitachi

Dominator

Penitentiary Pimp

Lil Pierre

Horror

Paranormal Whispers

Tributes

Nipsey Hussle Lockdown Society Tribute Dedication

Trayvon Martin; Injustice—If Trayvon Martin Could Talk

Kids' Books

Dear Bully

Todd the Amazon Turtle

Eagle & the Weasel Vol. I-IV

Education-Based/Personal Development

How to Love

How to Rap

How to Digital Detox

How to Tattoo & Start Up

How to Innovate

How to Avoid Burnout

How to Invest with Success

How to Become a Social Media Influencer & Creative

How to Start Own eCommerce Site & Business Online

How to Write a Book Template & Format

How to Write Corrective Emails with Successful Open Rates

How to Stop School & Mass Shootings; Dear Parents

How to Connect and Focus

How to Get Out of the Rat Race Post COVID-19

The Rich Mind Multiplier

How to Mind Shift; The Cognitive Switch

Personal Development

How to Life Coach; Plural Management

How to Read the Algorithm & Ride It

Incarcerated Lives Matter Movement; The Hitachi Choparazzi Blueprint

How to Google & SEO Results; Resource Tools

The Art of Manipulation Power of Persuasion & Sweet Science of Communication (Prevention Book)

Screenplays

Pimp of Da Ratchetts

Hot Thots

Top Notch

Eagle & the Weasel—Animation

Million Dollar Games

Weasel Society

* *

To help incarcerated author funding book projects for typeset, editing, cover designs, ISBN, STAN, Audibles, marketing, etc., the info would be provided at the About the Author page/bio of the book. Please help contribute to ILM and bring these books to life to help all ILM & BLM education and movements.

- Chapter 2 -

"ILM Movement"

My letter to all ILM Black women incarcerated that read this book or who can spread this reform blueprint ILM message. Who can share this book around the pod, or tier, or simply recommend it to someone you know in lockdown society...spread this ILM movement.

* * *

Dear Incarcerated Beautiful Black Woman,

The original woman...the oldest woman skull (Amy) was found in Africa. You all matter! Beyoncé says Black is King, I say Black is Queen, too. I care if nobody else don't care. I wanted to let my pen bleed the pain of the narrative the most underrated, unappreciated Black incarcerated women have attached with the stigma and dogmas.

You women are never forgotten and represent the ultimate struggle. It is 10x harder for a Black woman in society, especially from the streets or projects. All the use and abuse you suffered from since a young girl and tender age that you still struggle thru to this day. Still being raped, abused inside these institutions and sexually harassed daily by staff that goes under the rug. Also being railroaded at court into trumped-up charges and blotched plea agreements, too. You all matter! Victims of the criminal justice mass incarceration system.

I want y'all to know I got all the female facilities that want to reform seeking change and new skillsets. A blueprint to follow. I also will be able to speak, coach, and mentor at facilities and assist you with the same self-reform principles that helped my transition from the inside doing a complete 180-degree turnaround. Me and so many others. All living proof of opportunity and growth. Self-reflection.

It's August of 2020 and we praying Joe Biden pick a Black woman Vice President. However, I want y'all to know, you, too, can be presidents! Not just proud moms, but presidents of your family, community, and organizations. You can still be president of whatever you want. Also still get out and do whatever you want, including helping other girls transition to find their superpower to be a super Black woman! It don't have to wait until you get out, you can start now from within. Success takes steps! You can do it, 1000 percent. I am sure of that and you. You know why? Your heart still beating and you still breathing!

Y'all creators of not just life, but of self. Tap in to inner self. Uniqueness is at your fingertips, like your own unique thumbprints. I challenge you to pull out the resources within. Visualize.

Your personality and individuality is priceless and innate within, that nobody else in the world can do or articulate and use like you do exclusively. That you excel and are really great at! We, and the whole world, are waiting on you to reform and share your ultimate gift and superpower. I believe in you! I can't wait to hear y'all shared success transform stories.

Teflon Luv!

#ILM #REFORM

Sincerely Yours Truly,

Hitachi Choparazzi

* * *

"I'm in the whale like Jonah...I'm building my ark like Noahh... Mannn..."—Hitachi Choparazzi #FreeHitachiChoparazzi 2020 Mixtape Vol. 2 Animated

I attempted to get my Billion Dollar Blueprint logos, brand, and website on Phoenix billboards. Once the company found out I was locked up, despite him liking my Billion Dollar Blueprint brand message and hot logos, he would not take my $2500 or answer my calls and emails. I next attempted to get on the Phoenix light rail train for a trailer wraparound with Billion Dollar Blueprint brand for $3500 per month. They wanted me to do at least 60 days so they won't pay labor to take the Billion Dollar blueprint wrap down, which their 30 days is actually only 25 days. I told him first I wanted to see the data analytics from my website traffic and sales or click-thru rates. I was not about to commit to something as a risk investment without proof of concept and numbers of profitability. They could've been running my train wrap non-essential business hours, rush hours, or high-volume traffic hours. Either way, it was a no-go because I found out the Italian guy from the billboard company was partners with the light rail guy, too. It's obvious he told his partner I was incarcerated.

That was around the same time my White typist dropped me, denying to work on my urban novels, saying they're too gritty. It all clicked!

Before I get into the framework and breakdown of the ILM movement, formally introducing it on my platform thru my writings from incarceration, please let me, too, share a quick story of realization of self.

One day I was in my creative writing process and morning ritual routine. Something got into my eye. I blinked it fast, blew into it, and rubbed it repeatedly to no avail. I jumped up and ran into the mirror to look and see what's in my eye and irritating it.

Once I got to the mirror, I seen myself finally for the first time. My eye was not red or even had nothing in it This was an actualization. I seen myself for who I actually am. I was handsome. I seen my light freckles that I always got made fun of when I was younger, they lit up and sparkled like glitter. Next I seen my black-reddish skin. I was glowing in enlightenment. Then I even noticed my natural curly eyelashes, too. I always in life paid fine close attention to detail, being a tattoo artist and author. This made me shout: You matter! Incarcerated Lives Matter! This was in 2017. For the first time in life, from one look in the mirror, I felt like I mattered. From New York to Nebraska and being in the criminal justice system all made me feel like I did not matter and I couldn't see myself, only the picture they painted of me. A thug, pimp, gangster, convict, badass, a fuck-up, and a menace to society, troubled and broken, until I saw self-value, self-worth, and past all those mental repression ornament tags hanging up in my subconscious like a Christmas tree that swung around and around repeatedly like a merry-go-round at a public park for kids. It's not just oppression we suffer from, it's repression. Also it's not just repression from others we suffer from, it's self-repression, too.

Therefore, after this experience it enabled me to add a new element and value of a visual effect and affirmation. I created an actual visual affirmation. The power of verbal affirmations are strong daily practices. However, try a visual one in the mirror and see the results and feel the power throughout your days and weeks steadfast. It's been a proven technique and tool for me personally, 46 books and counting. Self-actualization is the only key into truly connecting to your consciousness.

Now people ask me about ILM movement, like how can I stop 400 years of oppression, trauma, and mental anguish that plagues our minds passed down from generation to generation? I tell them they right, one man cannot clear everyone's mental. However, I know one man can give everyone a blueprint and tool to touch their own mental and tap into psyche to fix themselves. I know I cannot just move one person from the inside, but if I can start a movement from inside, it will move everyone outside to follow.

This is why my origin behind the ILM movement as a tool for people incarcerated to find self, a voice, and a united push. That can create a strong enough buzz and practice to break thru to end mass incarceration period. All these partially split jury convictions in states like Louisiana 10 to 2 un-unanimous jury pools need to be banned and reformed. Our skin should not be our sin. It's the root of inequality. All these wrongful convictions and incarcerations, all these excessive and illegal sentences, all these petty probation/parole violations need to all stop. Racial profiling and arrest, including jail time for unpaid fines, all need to stop. This is the concrete mix for mass incarceration, including a slew of other elements of mass incarceration I did not mention. The reason why they cannot and refuse to fix these issues because it would make these reform laws retroactive. Therefore, if they free me from my illegal executed sentence order, they would automatically free 100k other people incarcerated suffering from an illegal sentence, too. Or whatever else injustice.

The main underlying reason for this is money and America's greed. This is not rocket science to fly. This is still America's first sin they refuse to fix. They steal the taxpayer's citizen money to house and imprison inmates. Why are they getting rich? Where are all these billions going? Besides in private prisons and stocks. This is also the reason they build more prisons than schools or fix the roads or old neighborhoods. You have to first look at prisons as a business and incarceration as a commodity to understand and see thru my lens for reform. They look at us as a number and make us feel like we don't matter, just numbers only. This is exactly what it is all about—numbers. Just like livestock except we're human livestock and they are human trafficking 101. The Senate and lawmakers House of Representatives know it, but they segue it, dehumanizing us as criminals. Really it was a loophole to encapture the wild untamed Negros back in the post-Lincoln days. Still to this day and our timeline, it's used as a way to enslave us technically. Therefore, the slave trade still exists. Read the constitutional amendments and tap in. All the Black family lives affected and broken apart by it from generations know this realization and woke but broke, helpless, devastated. Whereas, the people too bougie or disconnected cannot relate or have empathy towards incarcerated lives because they bought into the new society norms, narratives, or blinded by the same way the lady icon of justice blindfolded with a balancing weigh scale in her hand. We all from the same tribe and descendants of slaves. Our blood and bones are all throughout these American lands. Some Black people actually believe we weren't never slaves because they were never enslaved in the present day. Same people saying they do not believe coronavirus/COVID-19 is real. Same people also claim they

#woke! These are the same people that we need not to give our power or energy entertaining. Let's focus on us pushing together under one umbrella and cause for reform to end mass incarceration and police reform systemic racism. We all integrated, but mentally segregated.

The reason why I call myself the human Google is because of my mind and how it processes. Being incarcerated and in tune, I've learnt how to tap into my mind, no hacks. I discovered my superpower is my mind, and my mind is my supercomputer. This is how it works using both left and right brain hemisphere. Like Google searches typing in keywords for SEO (Search Engine Optimization) by optimizing, I, too, use pictures, memory, my senses, and emotions to search and pick my brain. By retrieving information from my brain, opposite of what the average person does. Instead of using Google to search and learn, I use my brain to search being incarcerated and developed a huge hippocampus memory structure in my brain that created a great habit. Nowadays people are too codependent on Google to retrieve info they already know but too lazy to seek. Relying on smartphones, apps, SEO, and computers versus searching within. Most people cannot remember their grandparents' number or 3 numbers stored in their contacts. It's true and I share this info with you to teach so you can learn. Again, this is how I was enabled to write 46 books, child safety devices, training videos, programs, apps, and so much more. An engineer and architect.

Now let's push consciously and truly woke with the acknowledgement of self, all Black and incarcerated lives. Nobody gets left behind. I need everyone's effort and undivided push to assist breaking these chains and unlocking doors and gates. We are about to attack and challenge these laws and mass incarceration to free people to connect back with their loved ones and society. These are our mothers, leaders, and next breakthrough artists. Let's now go over what I have bestowed in them from the inside with the ILM movement. Remember, you cannot be fully woke out there until you woke to what's going on in here with mass incarceration. The data is there, just use your phone. Black men and women are 5x more likely to get stopped by police, arrested, or harassed; 1 out of 4 is victim to police misconduct or brutality. We cannot let our people in mass incarceration rot, and the ones that did unjustly we need to break thru and reform that they did not rot in vain, either.

This book is not to move Oprah or JayZ, but to remove future generations from these vicious chains of mass incarceration and self-destruction vicious cycles. I represent the struggle inside here and out there, too. A megaphone thru my books for ILM and people that feel like they don't matter or lost in the penal system.

One day I caught an ET (Eric Thomas) video. He said we matter, and what we do matters. He talked about not knowing or having his biological father and being disconnected. This outward affected him and me along with so many others, including women, girls, little boys, and men. We all look for our father's security blanket, guidance, and his love. You don't feel appreciated or like you matter. Indirectly, it shows and reflects as a child and manifests as an adult, too. Even if people don't talk about it or express their void and feelings, it still silently exists. Suffering from the sins of our fathers.

My father made me, too, feel like I didn't matter. The same narrative society, police, and bias inequality put on me like it's impossible to matter because I can't, which, again, this same narrative plagues the urban community and germinates fuck-it attitudes with no filters. Shooting and polluting our neighborhoods outward hurt emotional infliction. Remember, anger and aggravation is an emotion, too. I know it all stems from a hurt place because I, too, been a victim and guilty of it. We must reverse our environment restraints regardless of the condition to make you feel like you worthless, lost hope, or don't matter. People only lash out just like a kid because they are angry, hurt, or lost. They can't relate and resolve their pain and problems, so they do what they know and reciprocate the same pain inflicting trauma to others, including family. It's usually nothing the matter with them. They lost or stuck in transition. They don't know how to shift or drive, period. They need help to wake and rise. They, too, are victims of their environment, awaiting for someone to assist them with a transition blueprint. The drugs and mental health are all issues that can be corrected and better implementations if people truly direct the time, energy, and all available resources. You can choose to not let your environment structure your mental environment and free yourself. You have to own and acknowledge it first, then you can take action.

Just like me, my whole life I just needed a role model, mentor, or positive structure to follow. Most kids just like me, too. If you be hands-on to show them right and realness with dedication early on without giving up on them, correcting them until they start to autocorrect themselves. Again, sometimes we have to go thru it to grow thru. In this book you will hear me repeat my messages in different methods because it ciphers in all the formulas. The reiteration is to beat the message in to change the narration. It's our ideology to many who don't have a chance to sit down, express ourselves, and make our voices be very loud and heard. Also, our push to transparency for change, and a chance to spotlight that we incarcerated matter, too. The flip side of the coin of police racial profiling and misconduct. We not internet memes. People laugh and diss us as jail memes. However, we real and human. They tie that criminal title around our necks to dehumanize us into the culture. Being dehumanized, Michelle Obama talks recently about low-grade depression. From Trump trauma, his rants, tweets, lies, bigotry, racist comments, and promotion of it, also violence. The ongoing protest and civil unrest. America in 2020 is a mess, welcome to our America where we been feeling dehumanized and a higher grade of depression, oppression, and repression.

ILM is to create a space for us to have a voice, be heard, have input, a dialogue, and social psychology. Mass incarceration, prosecutor misconduct, criminal justice reform are main topics and push. One case and step at a time is how change is made and progress is started.

The aim is to appeal to and impact lockdown society. Show them ILM, inspire, and lead by excellence. Spread awareness thru the institutions and this blueprint movement, too. Give them a proud voice and means to get their stories, greatness, craft, education, and skillsets out. For real reform and to transform their lives with perpetual growth to overcome obstacles and conquer challenges with self-discipline and dedication.

Even after they are released to help reintegrate with new skills, self-development, or a trade. A writing career is even possible. Again, this is why I chose to write all these self-development books and wanted to create a #1 library niche to help all people incarcerated on the inside read to catch up to speed, learn, educate, grow, build, reform, and resonate that don't have the resources, support, love, mentor, and means to assist with their transition. I been there to know what most people see and need to fix or work on. Therefore, I know what effective solutions work and how to troubleshoot and problem solve anything or outcome. That's why these self-development books are my contribution. I cannot wait to teach them on a broad scale once released to connect it with the world and tap directly into those in need. I love to teach and share my knowledge and blueprints to help the next person paying it forward and down the generations. Also inspire people incarcerated to become great and evolve forward into their greatness.

"Never doubt a person or that an incarcerated person can move the world out and forward from within with the power of the mighty pen." —Hitachi Choparazzi

Let's get deeper into the logics of the ILM movement. ILM and lockdown society movement is a movement with incarcerated lives from the inside to bring transparency, spread awareness, prison reform, and self-reform. We woke and self-conscious, each one teach one, rehabilitation and growth.

You guys working out there, we working and pushing a hard line inside here. Starting with ourselves accountability, support mentally, spiritually, and brotherly love. The old-fashioned way, the gangs are in sync and in order. It's not a war on the inside like the war outside on the streets for a reason. It's all alliance and reform. Self-reform starts within us and lifting up others. The ability to impact and inspire each other with the formula to reverse their time and turn it into a positive to rebuild self is a very essential key. This is the inception process that enables them to transition. Plant the seed and they will water it. It takes longer for some seeds to grow. However, long as it's germinating, eventually they will blossom and bear righteous abundant fruit.

They say the lotus flower grows in the mud, the more deeper the mud, the more beautiful the flower. Now, how long do you think it takes for the germinating process with a lotus seed in thick mud? Eventually it will grow, right? Exactly! This is exactly my methodology with ILM movement. Eventually, it will grow after it spreads and germinates.

Again, I extract value from the pen out of nothing, just by extracting resources from within self. Using prison as a platform to build and reform self. This is another applicable principle that ILM movement follows.

We are the forgotten and government slaves out of sight, out of mind like the dead. Disconnected from society and our loved ones. We all get muzzled and swept under the rug our cases, arrest, injustices, and incarcerations with no voice and able to actually speak out. It's a single battle. No helps, means, support systems, or resources and people to look over the data of arresting officers, biased judges, prosecutors, and sellout lawyers, which all part of this systemic racism that's the leading cause of mass incarceration.

Let's start a convo about ILM and help change narratives. A change in criminal justice system and prison reform bills is all possible to end mass incarceration. However, it begins with us and our push both ILM and BLM movements. Total connectedness and changes potential and awareness to crack it. We cannot give up on the perpetual push.

Let me repeat this with emphasis on it. At Rayshard Brooks' funeral Reverend Warnock said God has a record of using people with a record, also don't dismiss people just because they have a record, including prophets from the Bible that committed crimes and were incarcerated. Even Jesus was imprisoned before he was racially prosecuted and executed.

Therefore, again, you cannot continue to overlook people incarcerated or convicted and discredit them. Their validation can matter and influence the most or mass, too.

If you did not catch Rayshard Brooks' interview with Reconnect Fresh Out, he talked about reentry, his kids' disconnect and a new life, fresh start, including job placement.

Rayshard Brooks, Breonna Taylor, and George Floyd is a representation of us all of color and connection. That is proof on and off camera, the police and systemic racism is the problem. Inequality. They are the hunters that throw us on the modern-day auction block system to be monetized, which the Constitution amendment states slavery shall be abolished except for government slaves.

Throwing us in a grave or a cage. The inception of the police were to catch slaves before community police existed.

Massive incarceration is never-ending slave trade. The U.S. is the #1 place in the world for mass incarceration. Why is that? It's because they are getting paid billions per year taxpayer-funded to warehouse inmates, which majority population is Black men and women of all ages, including juveniles. They beyond stereotype us, they marketplace us. All while painting that criminal illusion picture effect, pluralizing and typecasting all of us into one neat category. You still not woke yet, this is only Chapter 2, it's plenty more to help rub clear your lenses to.

I want all of us to have a plural vision with ILM that 100 years from now in 2120 it would be frowned upon and looked down upon mass incarceration like slavery to a broken system. By us all pushing as a whole to have a sure breakthrough with a thorough prison reform bill passed. Not saying Senator Corey Booker is not trying with his prison reform bill. Also we need a racial bias data system in place to weave out all the prejudice in the criminal justice system germinating massive incarceration. Check out any patterns, from ethics, misconduct, behavior traits of excessive sentence patterns, too.

From the judge, police, prosecutors, district attorneys, lawyers to the corrections, all have stock shareholders behind the public scenes. All in mass incarceration, private prisons entities, and commodities. It's heavy behind the scenes and more than meets the blind eyes. They train and promote the public to denounce us and look at us all as criminals and thugs, to turn their backs and a blind eye on us. Hiding the underlying truth that's problematic and a cash cow.

Realize time is money; the more time they give out, the more money they get back, which means the more money they pocket and grease official palms with, too. Monetize and capitalize. Plus ignited with underlying racism is their generational institutional system.

People in massive incarceration slavery and system slavery all suffer from true inequality. Systems of slavery like music, business, publishers, contracts, etc. People seek financial freedom, spiritual freedom, and liberty like America's Constitution emphasizes.

The Constitution is supposed to be a guide and liberty. It's supposed to be fair, too. The Constitution was built on philosophy and politics. The question to ask the Constitution, is there a rationality to it, and of what was being opposed? You want to be able to stand with the people, stand with the protestors and youth. Politicians cannot stand with the people. That's why they cannot understand the people on these race relations, police, and prison reform issues. It shouldn't take different ploys of protest, demonstrating, or even cries of violence to strike their attention for reform or ILM and BLM. You got to be able to cross over in both worlds and bridge the gap. Non-leaders follow the leaders. This is why Trump is following Twitter instead of the people to lead their demands righteous and settle their disputes. He was supposed to be working on prison reform with Kim Kardashian, which we still have yet to see a real reform bill pass and hundreds of thousands free!

Free the slaves with prison reform over 1 million Black men and women, with mass incarceration majority of the ones inside is woke self-conscious. We don't have successful tools and programs to help build further on their new growth, drug rehab, and spiritual awareness with their newfound inside transition they learnt in lockdown society. Then after they get out to no outside resources at their fingertips, and true support to help them reset and reestablish a successful reentry like Rayshard Brooks reiterated. Some people been locked up so long, they don't know how to text or work a smartphone and get online, seriously. Also it's a mission fresh out to get interviews without lying about your history or prior work history timeline absence, and to get jobs successfully or housing. The housing is the main issue. People upon reentry do not have housing placement and repeat offenders being right back into them streets. Plus society banishes them and plays into the narrative and psyche of systemic racism indirectly brainwash and banishment. People really play into that psychology of that's on them and they not my people or family, only thugs on drugs. Makes us shake our heads as people turn on us.

Friends, family, and society all disconnect, outcast, or exile ex-cons upon reentry and almost forgotten, like the living dead walking among the living but dead to the world.

The true aim is hands down wholeheartedly to diminish the Constitution amendment allowing these government slaves. Rewrite the language, reform the system and narrative of a Black incarcerated livestock money market monopoly. Reestablish rehab ways and implement better programs, especially drugs and mental health, versus cages like dog kennels. Relinquish these cages, shackles, and chains.

Again, you can hear the dead crying out from the grave, but you cannot hear the incarcerated echoes from the cage? ILM, too. Why doesn't society acknowledge the injustices, mass incarceration, and systemic racism in the penal broken system?

Police misconduct and racism they view us as another one off the streets or dead. Then let the racist and highly biased judicial system hang us high. Drug charges are leading cause of mass incarceration and excessive sentences. However, the majority of the drugs isn't manufactured in the U.S.

Systemic oppressor judicial system. We all suffer from generational racial trauma dating back since 1619 days of enslavement. We can't go back to sweeping it under a rug if we all woke, right? Or people turning their backs and a blind eye on a million incarcerated Black lives, Hispanic lives, too. This book applies to all, and universal for White privilege, non-privilege, all people of color or non-color. All people incarcerated and people free. This book is not a challenge. It's to spread awareness, shine a spotlight, to unite and break thru change for both sides out there and inside here, too. Let's push reform.

We cannot ignore the fundamental miscarriage of justice. The district attorneys and detectives across the nation coerce, threaten witnesses to lock them up if they don't comply, testify, or point people out by force. Innocent people locked up or on death row, illegal sentences and convictions, excessive sentences, felony murder, conspiracy clauses, and alleging historical priors against you to enhance your sentence after paying debt to society for it already, 3 strikes, needs all to be broken up and reformed. If we want to end mass incarceration, we have to address and correct these main issues, including racism and racial profiling. It's algorithms for everything else but mass incarceration reform.

The system don't want to acknowledge or correct its mistakes. Just like the Oklahoma Julius Jones case and many more fighting for their innocence. Therefore, it is up to us as a whole to push together ILM and BLM movement and connect because if they Black, they are your brother and sister, the same tribe. I am my brother's and sister's keeper. I can tell you from personal experience losing my brother Pierre/Peppy at a young age and homies that were more like brothers from another mother to me. Their deaths crushed me, and life sentences did, too.

Being born on a plantation or the projects and hood, you are already targeted and subject to death or modern slavery. Marked by the same police sworn to protect and serve. Penitentiaries are the new plantations. You do not have to be inside here with me to experience it, you just simply got to be woke to see it.

This is why I founded this ILM and lockdown society movement inside, and the face of it and reform because I am living it. It's my mentality and lifestyle. A reformer, leader, and advocate with a blueprint!

- Chapter 3 -

ILM & Lockdown Society Blueprint"

People would see all my book covers, pics of foreign cars, and pics of Egypt, Puerto Rico, Jamaica, Brazil from my cousin traveling and would be awed with eyes wide. They would come to my cell and ask how do they level up and get on their blueprint, too? Or how to find theirs? Even at chow hall or on the rec yard, they would be grouping up by the dozens around me seeking knowledge, wisdom, and how-tos. I wasn't the self-proclaimed how-to guru, that's what everyone else called me in lockdown society. The C.O.s would see this and hate my progress, status, and attempt to break the crowds, hating or automatically think we plotting mastermind facility control. Just simply silliness, however. Every time you have a newfound energy, it creates a portal hole and breakthrough. I had all the undivided attention, including the wrong attention from Corrections and their investigating special units. I did not care or sweat it because real and truth always win and prevail. I got back to my same ole 2-step.

The ILM Blueprint is for all men, women, and juveniles in lockdown society seeking change and self-reform to implement. I don't have a high 150 I.Q. like Edison or Einstein. Mine is 130. However, my I.Q. on connectedness is 150 like theirs. Why do you think these billionaires have a super secret recipe? I've all the possessive qualities and human traits they have, just like you do, too We all human. Why do you think it's not a Black Jeff Bezos, Elon Musk, Mark Zuckerberg, Steve Jobs, Bill Gates, or Warren Buffett? Even though it's highly possible, we lost in the sauce and too busy chasing our tails, disengaged and disconnected. We hating on each other, selfish, stealing from each other, or killing each other. Remember the pyramids in Egypt and that it's part of Africa that we were kings and queens and ruled for centuries on end before we got enslaved and stripped of our names, freedom, religion, and history. We adopted all European ways, but we did not adopt all the European successful ways and connectedness. A White man named Willie Lynch wrote an actual blueprint for the Negro slaves to turn the light against the dark, break them mentally and physically like they would a mule or a horse in comparison. Then he would play on the Black woman psyche to strip her down with torturing the Black man in front of her so she will actually bestow fear in her son and offspring to fear and be in compliance. This what he called to tame a Negro and kill the untamable ones. It's sad but true. You must do your own research to see all the gruesome details.

Therefore, I decided to do an ILM Blueprint to enable all Negros still enslaved to a Constitution, institution, and self. Even though a lot of us perpetuate Willie Lynch's theory and blueprint with sociological and psychological effects indirectly. The majority is even lost and not woke to this notion.

I've always had an innate profound gift with people and pushing my energy tapping to make direct connection. I've a strong spirit and a good dude with big heart of vibrations meaning I feel and pass energy off vibes. Remember, everything in the universe, your body is all constantly moving in motion or vibrant. This total connectedness or a universal connection that's called different names like astral body, super conscious, God mind, level 4 connectedness, etc. However, I am able to relate, reshape, and reform anyone being around me. Give me 8 hours per day for one whole week and I guarantee you will see instant change in that individual, including people with ADHD, bipolar, depression, suicidal, or SMI (serious mental illness).

I tell you guys this from true experience being inside where all the outcasts reside. It's people in here that need help and suffer serious mental disease versus caged up and in jail. They need attention, to be heard, loved, or simply helped. Old Man Duke was clinically cleared insane. He would hear voices talk back to them and walk in high knee steps with his pants pulled all the way up to his chest. He was intimidating to staff and inmates, standing 6'4", 250 lbs. One day at the rec yard, Old Man Duke was in the corner, talking to himself. I pardoned myself before intervening into Duke's conversation. I asked Duke if he didn't mind taking a walk with me. He told me hell nawh (no), that he didn't trust pimps! I chuckled and smiled at Old Man Duke and told him I'm not a pimp, I am a man! Then I offered him a smoke, tossed a rollie and a Snickers candy bar. As Duke caught the smoke and snatched the Snickers like no tradeback, I said in a stern voice, "Duke, I know you didn't do it." Duke's eyes grew wide and pupils dilated a little in the AZ bright sunshine. First words came out of Duke's mouth in reply was, "They lied on me," and hell nawh he did not do shit. I shook my head and told Duke let's walk and talk about it. I cut Duke's hair that rec yard afternoon and brought him back to life, knocking that old-man gray up off him. That day was the start of our friendship.

Old Man Duke would stand outside my door like a security guard. He would wait for me going to chow or anywhere. He would tell people, "Pimpin writing, he busy," and clothesline someone who went past go and his wishes. The staff would hate it but wouldn't dare mess with

Old Man Duke outside my cell front. The cons would say Pimpin in a prison pickle and got him a nutty sidekick jokingly. I would correct them and say Duke not crazy, he just operates on a different frequency that you guys cannot get on. Me and Old Man Duke vibed till he died. I didn't cry because Duke lived and was tired and lonely in this world and institution. He was disconnected from his family and life. That's why he would talk to himself because nobody else would take the time to talk to him. Empathy. Even Duke's family wrote him off as crazy and gave up on him. No calls, visits, or letters and pictures. I gave Old Man Duke peace because I made him finally feel like he mattered. To Duke I was his BF (best friend). Notice I never tried to force Duke into a society perception of norm. I corrected him once, but he still called me Pimpin. In his mind that's who I was. It was okay because Duke just had a perception of me stuck in his head, even though I knew who I was as a man reformed that did a 180 turnaround. He just did what society did to him, framing him as crazy instead of really tapping into him. If Duke would've got the proper help as a child before his mind perception warped and disconnected him from his loved ones and society frequencies.

I have always had this gift of gravitation, vibrations, energy, and connectedness from peoples, kids, pets, and parents or family, period. It also was a younger SMI guy named Fitzgerald. Everyone would shoo him away like a pesty fly and say, "Fitzgerald, get out of here. You know you crazy like that glue!" I was the only one on the compound to break through to Fitzgerald and connect, too. He was really more like radio and autistic. He would be humming and bust out laughing or if you try to talk to him, he would look at you silly and bust out laughing harder.

I figured since he laughed all the time, I would tap in with a different approach sternly. Like a father figure and a little bossy approach. I would demand Fitzgerald in a harsh shout tone. Not yelling, but firmly to get his attention. He knew I meant business. I would make eye contact even when he attempted to avoid it. I'd turn him back around and tell him, "Fitzgerald, you not crazy like glue—make your bed, brush your teeth, and go take you a shower, then put some deodorant on!" He would comply and I would cut his hair, too. I was his accountability partner and coach. At first I would get on Fitzgerald about 3 to 4 times a day. Then 50-odd days later, he would always have his bed made and room clean and the first one to shower. Now, getting Fitzgerald to truly wash his hair was a totally different task. He had a baby afro that was matted but looked like dreadlocks. I would taper cut it and leave his mini afro. I wasn't getting paid to help take care of Fitzgerald by the state, like people that's caretakers get on the outside, nor do I want it. What I want is to know why these people with mental health problems or disabilities are caged in a high level 4 yard or max custody because don't nobody want to deal with them. I could write a hundred books on this issue and all the people I helped this 11-and-a-half years in lockdown society. Fitzgerald's mom and sister thanked me for trimming his hair. They gave my son a soda and vending machine items to take to my table. I gladly declined and told my son to ask them to tell Fitzgerald to relax before he gets my cell searched. After Fitzgerald started doing things on his own independently, I would reward him with my burner phone and let him watch my Triller videos. He would laugh and play them on repeat, screaming Hitachi-Hitachi-Hitachi very animated. He was doing this in the visitation room having an episode when he seen me. My son was crying laughing.

It is also the same way how I shared in previous chapters how my mind works like a human Google and tapping in to retrieve info from life stored in my memory hippocampus. I will teach you how to tap in, too, and the technical breakdown.

First, let's enable you with ILM Blueprint to help you level self up. Then you will be able to find you and discover your innate natural superpowers and gifts.

ILM Blueprint premise is about 2 things: transformation with an end goal of self-reformation. It's a devoted daily practice and process to build this new habit, mentality, and prominent lifestyle.

Next, apply these principles with your heart and head centered. To enable or activate your ILM Blueprint transformation and reform, you need to get familiar with all these underlying principles. Education, by educating yourself such as reading, watching, learning always to better self. Elevation, rising, energy vibrations and shift. Like administry change of energy, reverse field of energy, and pushing the envelope. Innovation, new ways of implementation of self, and challenging yourself to renew thinking process. Self-discipline, intellectual, mental, physical. Self-impose accountability, will, and work ethics. Development, skillsets, applying different methodology working for discovery, study this blueprint to become more diverse. Self-awareness, consciousness, meditation, a higher realm of transparency level, enlightenment, empowered, and awaken.

Last principle is health, conscious eating and exercising regularly, which is the most important because without health, you cannot have wealth. It's 2 types of wealth. Wealth is spirit, or accumulated wealth. Health food conscious and choices like going vegan, plant-based diets, or simply organic. All junk food and fast food is bad for your health with diabetics or hypertension. It's all artificial additives consisting of salts, sugars, trans fats, saturated fats, and fructose corn syrup. All non-organic food and vegetables can have pesticides sprayed or steroids and fertilizer. Even their massive production of food like livestock cows, pigs, chicken, etc., all get injected with hormones, steroids, vitamins, and antibiotics to prevent a mass production outbreak within the animals. This is why people developing cancer at record-breaking speeds and underlying health issues. Some people can't even use prescribed antibiotics because they immune from the food they ate of massive production. Being incarcerated, you cannot really eat too organic and healthy with fresh fruit and vegetables. However, you can be health food conscious by all the junk food on the commissary list. All the ramen noodles, chips, candy is all junk. High sugar and salt, etc.

Let's go back over the ILM Blueprint principles for transformation and self-reform. They are education, elevation, self-awareness, innovation, self-discipline, development, health consciousness. To be present, self-organize inside to tap in your mind and consciousness. Change regular state to recalibrate all the things that're attached to these conditions to believe how limited we are. We need to peel those layers off to be coherent in mind and heart. Living in stress or harsh conditions will release stress hormones cortisol or serotonin. You can't sustain change if you're incoherent. Meditation to reset helps you to tap in to become focused, consciousness, and awareness. To get you on track to connect. Taking your attention off surroundings and material stuff, which that is the bridge to the quantum field. The inner experience of the way we see the world and wake up. ILM feels undervalued and overlooked. You need to be so aware you won't let that behavior run you. Observe that thought that you program into your mental or better known as your subconscious. Then become conscious of those hardwired unconscious thoughts. If you do not know the difference between your subconscious and consciousness, subconscious is existing in the mind without entering to conscious awareness. Also below the threshold of consciousness. Basically being unaware. Your subconscious is your automated processed program without thinking, like being in autopilot all day. Whereas, consciousness is to be aware. Mentally awake or alert. Not sleep or unconscious. Done with awareness or purpose. Known or felt by one's inner self. This is what all those hashtags stamped woke is saying they are basically conscious.

You need belief and to reprogram yourself for growth and transformation. Remember, you all have value and economical empowerment. Society tells you that you don't have value or you don't have education piece of paper to get the job when really you have a technical skill that only you specialize in and just need a chance to showcase and prove work ethics. Do work course development programs of paradigms. Then you can help make history by reforming, breaking, and changing history. The humanity paradigms breakdowns are racism, politically, socially, educational, and health.

The beam is what you want to get under. The fulcrum is the how-to. Then self-regulate, don't allow people or things outcome to control you. Then create something amazing and better from within you. The world needs more resources and innovators. Need more models to practice and get out of a pickle.

Now before we get into an ILM Blueprint discovery and fundamental development session, I want to share this with you real quick. They say never teach someone something because they will outdo you and beat you out. The same student and master teaching principle. The master never shows the student all what he knows, therefore he could never be defeated because he never reveals his flaws even though he old as dirt. I strongly disagree. I believe in teaching all and passing knowledge down generations to make progress, and eventually someone breaks through for relief for all, including the following generations. Therefore, feel free to reread this, write down all tips, notes, and principles you need to work on to challenge or better self. Or listen to this Audible book over as needed and chapters that apply.

Who can organize dysfunction and chaos? Me, because I come from it, and it's my background. That's how I am able to develop creative methods of implementations and tools to enable us all. Plus I always lead by my actions, work ethic, mental, and love from my heart from me to you to connect. Remember this: marketing is influencing. The only way to influence people is to explain something to them. Also impression. Explain how, what, and why to take action. Relevance and significance.

This ILM Blueprint is about optimization. Optimize your life like a Google search engine. It's a personal lifelong of optimization. I can take what most people cannot describe and bring it vivid/clear. Simply concepts. Make it easier for people to grasp or learn and implement. This is one of my many discovered superpowers thru this ILM Blueprint formula for reform I am sharing with you.

You can do, too. Every skill is learnable with practice and dedication like Kobe. Build energy in life on your desires. Even conflict or trauma that builds your core behind your push of success. Remember, you absolutely have to humble your ego first. Else you will crash and burn without getting over that curve to tap into your infinite potential. Next, master yourself. Your belief should be I will and I deserve. That unwilling belief or self-worth needs to impregnate your brain, regardless of people that make you feel like you don't matter.

Let's use a scenario example. Say if you ladies in female facilities and desire to seek reform by implementing the ILM Blueprint, you create a desire you want the outcome for as a catalyst to push you forward, even sparking creativity. You would use prison as your muse or platform to launch and push you for betterment. Then attach your daughter or kids to the end reward. Everything that comes into existence must go out of existence. You can lose your focus, momentum, sight, and vision of your goals and simply distractions. Focus on your daughter's homecoming, use gratitude to keep you grounded inside that you still breathing, alive, and healthy with a second chance at life eventually. You will gain more than you ever lost being new and found with energy.

Create an awareness and playlist of routines to keep you moving forward. Like a shark, don't go or swim backwards. You must develop a shark mentality to conquer self.

If you change your perception, you change your life with the will to. It's will that is very important. Click down is finding value out of keywords in sentences. Asking yourself why is that so important, because if you catch the keywords you say in use in your sentences, you will catch the root of your patterns, pain, problems to solve. You will begin to be more self-conscious, thinking before you speak or react, which helps you find self and core values. The whole essence of transformation in the power of your tongue.

Actions, take your core value, implicate it, and you can even monetize it or them into skillsets. Your job is to find it and keep trying new things. Also, outrage. You have something that outrages you and again, use this as a trigger to push or spark creativity, too. Value your passion, what you love to do, your freedom mentally, and new connections. Great leaders are all triggered or pissed off, and use pain points as their motive to push. Just look at some of the greatest discoveries in history. This is what I mean by reversing your time, whether incarcerated or in quarantine, to work for you versus against you. Also prison as your pain point to pivot and platform off of. With this framework, you, too, can tap in and find greatness. It's also reverse engineering like some of the greats used to implement since the beginning of the human brain thousands of years ago.

Therefore, hold your core values that you possess and dear to you, outrage, and awareness. With tension, you have to keep it, because it keeps you whole and motivated, pushing hard at achievement. Feeling is concentration and vibration, like I explained earlier with Old Man Duke. Concentration gives focus of energy. Use your faculties, higher faculties, to use them like intuition. Intuition is attention and vibration. You must tap into their energy.

You following people wasting time and your life instead of following yourself and discover your innate blueprint. Nowadays people know others better than themselves. Following social media personalities and validating likes, however, don't follow their own personality or truly like and know it. All reform is reflection of inner change. Reforming self is a love language once you fine-tune self, which will equal perpetual success. Remember, success isn't nothing but an innate elegant love story. This is why people are infatuated and obsessed with success and chase it, overlapping in the human rat race for first place.

You can do it your blueprint with success your response, stimulus, thinking, and thought. Put it into your subconscious mind to implement. Simply speak it into existence, and your mind will begin to initiate the process of manifesting what you will into a reality. You have to still tap in, focus your energy and time on building it like the snowball effect.

It's all mental tools and scooping ideas to existence. Implementation, action, and execution. It shouldn't be no mental blocks; if so, kill your ego and dig in deeper. Emotions need to be let go of. Don't sweat the small stuff or hold on to the past. Past hurt, pain, betrayal, and mistrust. Live in the present and be present to self and life. Plan forward and live forward with that shark forward progress mentality. Thinking is the most important. The consequence value in thinking is priceless.

You are trying to activate your outer activity when you haven't activated your inner. It's a fundamental flaw. Goal generation, meaning you're interested in the fruit, not the actual tree. The only quality is clarity. They have loud mouths and proud advertising demand because they have merely confidence and not clarity. It's whatever you have perceived. Perception is their expression and not actions. It's all conceptional and not perceptional. The accumulation for information. It's only 5 senses of perception. It's 3 types of learning you can use: auditory, visual, and kinetic. You may be a faster or a better learner with only one of these. It really doesn't matter long as you can learn things effectively and implement. Once you get it down pat, you can share or teach others and pay it forward to add value and make value. This truly is self-worth and self-value.

I have really been around and have actual experience with SMI, bad-asses, pure egotistic, narcissists, etc. I can get thru to them all with short time and have them implement the blueprint principles to reform and find self. Again, thru energy and total connectedness to the universe.

Penetrate ego. We let our ego lead and tell us don't, won't, and can't change. Egos say Hell No to change, but it's not in charge or control if you're conscious of it and being the seat of your emotional impulses.

You need to refocus and connect to your frontal lobe. Your ego is in charge of your fight or flight and to assess risk. It's risk management, but you give it a vicious voice with all bark, no bite.

Well, I am here to help you fracture that fragile ego and reverse the effect to take back your control and connect to not just self, but to the vibrations of the universe. Just like I do from a 6x8 jail cell writing what you feel and need for your heart and eardrums to soothe your brain with realness pure and sincere from my heart to yours. Reflecting and pushing back out power and infinite intelligence into the universal laws of the ancient land frequencies.

Therefore, people don't realize they have a choice or choices. We create our own bars and imprison ourselves. It heightens levels of energy and awareness. An enduring state by trigger and challenge and engage. Oxygen and blood flow. The concept of flow.

Enthusiasm is key and looking forward to something again incarcerated, like by simple choices, discipline, and habits. Purpose and progress are the magic and life we all deserve. Empowers and empowerment with achievement and implementation to all. Mind, body, and spirit optimization. Total self-awareness and optimizing your life independently, not codependent on others, or institution narratives that they put into your subconscious indirectly to stick. Then your body and actions will implement it.

People don't like things that confront or challenge their ego. This is what I was doing with Fitzgerald, challenging him firmly to make up his bed and shower, to take care of his personal hygiene like a child because he had a child mentality. Another prime example of challenging or confronting someone's ego is Jon Taffer off of the reality TV show Bar Rescue. He challenges and confronts the bar owners' and staff members' egos. He calls them out and yells to drill thru to crack their egos down. Once he shatters their ego with a reality check, he gets them to do a turnaround and take action to implement betterment and a successful establishment. It's simple framework and structure. A lot of people didn't know or acknowledge their ego took over in the driver seat. Pride is all ego, too. My pride I couldn't let go of and the reason why I'm incarcerated, it was all ego.

Keep affirmation daily that's fixed in your mind like mantras. Thought waves penetrate thru space and energy. Paradigm is built genetic and environmental of the mind that the subconscious control and program. A paradigm is a model or pattern. It can also be a systematic inflection of a verb or noun showing complete conjugation or declension.

It's your conscious mind that has the intellect. It's there, but your subconscious mind programs it. Most of us come from broken home settings or dysfunctional backgrounds, which is an environmental paradigm. However, this doesn't mean you're exempt to change. Don't let that be a clutch and your excuse. Your program genetical conditions and your program environment conditions are both your inner paradigms to manage or break out of to prevail and overcome.

It never expresses it perfectly because of the subconscious paradigm. Paradigms get us to quit things because we're programmed. You must be able to see and change your paradigm. A culture is paradigm. A country, a business, all is a paradigm. A prison is a paradigm, too. We all come from stagnant paradigms or consist of paradigms in all forms to enable us with stress hormones and mental blocks like the maze runners. If you know what your paradigm is, change your behavior. Your only challenge is to find out what yours is by identifying it, then problem solve by fixing it. Again, autocorrect yourself.

Repression is to exclude from consciousness to restrain, suppress, curb, or subdue, like a painful memory. Repudiate is to disown, cast off, or refuse to have anything to do with. These both, repression and repudiation, are two things that we do to self or others do to us. Remember, your whole aim of this blueprint structure and principles is ultimate goal of self-reform. To the youth that does not understand what reform is, I'll break it down. My authentic message is to impact and mentor you with a reform process and what you learn thru my education thru storytelling. Reform is to make better or improve by removal of faults, or to correct or improve one's own character or habits. Now the reform we pushing for with prison and police reform is to improvement or correction of what is corrupt or defective.

People should study and have a mentor that already accomplished what you want to do. Have a goal and when you write it, have it already intellectual. The gestation period of spirit and the time we operate by law like sun, moon, and seasons. Love what you do, or be very passionate so you don't get burnout. Let it flow natural. If you love what you do, they say you'll never work a day in your life. When winners or scholars write history or education books, they never mention their failures, only their forward success and fulfilment formulas. This is why I attached all my personal failures and embarrassment in this book to give actualization and realization for reform that worked for me and can for you, too.

You cannot be indecisive. People fear the unknown or to step out your element into a new environment. Most people live in bondage because of fear. They don't understand it and stay in comfort zone. It's not just about principles and putting in work only. You must change your mindset and have mindfulness. People live in intellectual only and do not take action to achieve it.

If you work at little steps or pain each day or face a terror barrier daily, you getting emotionally involved to change your paradigm. Once you break thru the fear, you conquer and develop a new action or a good habit. It's hard to get back up from jail and self-reform from the inside without assistance, support, or a blueprint to know how. It takes effort and courage. I'm speaking for over a million people that cannot speak for themselves. Don't follow society's paradigms that pigeonhole you.

We have infinite potential, imagination, will, that you need to learn how to use them. Our perception has to be shifted. If you want to learn more, you got to go to someone who knows more. Remember, if you don't know much, you cannot do much. I am repeating myself so ILM reading this can grasp the ism, and I wire the blueprint in their mental to connect and apply for effective betterment. My point of view and reward is others' success is my success and blessings. My job is to help enable growth in people to take on bigger roles in their lives of personal development. Also inspiring people to evolve, elevate, and reform self with maximum optimization. Everyone incarcerated or in society needs to read, period. Little books have the biggest impact. You cannot be lazy or passive. If you don't like to read, watch videos, seminars, webinars, or Audibles. Audibles is the new reading, so while you driving home from work, please cut the music on your playlist off and create an Audible book playlist. Educate yourself, history, too. Growth and development.

Next we will get into our continued conversation about me tapping into my mind to work like human Google. The technical name and skillset is called superconscious mind capability. Napoleon Hill calls the super conscious mind infinite intelligence, how he describes it. Some people call it the God mind or God speed mentality. Super conscious mind capability flows like peak flow. With Super Conscious Mind

Capability, you tap into your genius and functions for your creativity. The genius trusts and believes in the value of their thoughts and ideas.

It automatically programs and solves the first problem and implement. Creativity cannot be forced. If you keep that clear mental picture, your goal will come. If you believe it will happen, then your goal will actually happen, even the impossible. Major breakthroughs come from people that have ideas, and not even in that field or profession have solutions.

Have the ability to see insight in a new way and source of all. It works non-conscious all day. Super conscious energy from the atmosphere, sometimes a crackling of ideas. It is triggered by clarity and decisiveness. It releases ideas, energy, and goals. Also positive affirmations and strong emotionalization triggers your super conscious mind energy.

Remember this because it's important. The super conscious mind capability will take a goal you think of and achieve it in the universe for a sure reality. Or it can enable us to teach people the essential lesson to achieve valuable lessons. When winners lose, they learn and keep going to achieve ultimate goals. This is what Kobe Bryant and Thomas Edison with the lightbulb mastered. Serendipity events to come together, and synchronization forms a pattern that comes together. Whereas, a limbic system cannot be duplicated.

The super conscious mind works when you're not thinking of it or concentrating on it. The degree and belief we have is how much we get out of it. If you put 8 percent in, you get 8 percent out. However, you can pre-program it. It has its own computer. You must immediately act on it or implement the flash that comes in from the super conscious mind and move on it quickly proactively. Sometimes these golden gems be within seconds and with abundance.

By simply plugging in and planting a mustard seed into the super conscious mind, you can achieve indeed, regardless of prior education, intellect, program, genre, etc. Whatever you put in your super conscious mind, you must put it out. Look at me. I couldn't read or write. Now I write personal development books and intellectual structures from my innate gifts and superpowers. I couldn't tell you what none of these words meant 12 years ago. I was able to think and move outside the box once they placed me in a concrete tomb box. All possible because of the super conscious mind and vibration frequencies I operate on that connected and are in sync with the universe and universal laws.

Keep your mind and focus on what exactly you want to happen. Laser focus because this is optimization just like the SEO Google. Make sure to systematically exclude all your fear, negative thoughts or energy, because you can revoke them. Don't read them, write them, or think about them. By immutable law, it will come into existence. This is what you do, hear, and say rubs off and mirrors you. Like if you see someone yawning or crying, it's so infectious you start to simultaneously. It's called mirror neurons. Avoid same toxic place environment, same toxic people, and same toxic things, or else you will most definitely get the same results for life.

Now, the neurological genetical energy connecting to your body to push. Transcendental energy field electric and spiritual arousal. The arousal of neuro from brain is not chemical, but to awaken your energy and perspectives wide view. You would be so aware and heightened with competence, you won't let that previous behavior run you.

Next on frequency you think. When you set a goal, you got to flip your frequency higher. Then you begin to attract all on that vibration. The primary law is vibrations, then attraction, and frequency. Set your mind on the frequency to attract what you need to attract. Live in the now. People use time and things for physical benefit. The entire process of your mental is gratitude. You have to show up with the same focus and intensity daily. The more you learn, the more you share. The more successful, the more humble. You need to practice humbling your ego or giving yourself an ego slap to get to tap into your potential and infinite intellect.

Happy, healthy, and wealthy in spirit. If I can win, anybody can win. It's about getting the right info to the right people or from the right people. It's true people do not know that they don't know and that they are lost or misguided. It's my job to help them find their right path and put the right directions to go. Super conscious capabilities, when it computes, it has ultimate access to all data to solve and store in subconscious mind. All creativity is improvement in any area. Even in restoration process, restoration justice helps heal. Those that pay money pay attention. Invest in yourself to tap in or create wealth. Remember, it takes intellectual discipline, too. Then teach people about themselves because most people don't know self or how to transition to reform. Get rid of excuses and execute exclusively. Harness your weakness into a strength. Live in demand of self.

Once you learn self and know thyself, your dopamine won't push and excite you for the overexcited outcome. If you can do things naturally without expecting the outcome attachment in exchange, like doing art or things just for the cash flow, but it's something you dislike and goes against your values or principles. I'll truly express and articulate it without being attached to the results or outcomes. Dopamine receptors is the reward chemical that adds or subtracts reward in the brain. Don't confuse your goals with visions.

It's no shortcuts. You must be willing to learn, fail, grow, and get better. If you don't play or see yourself as a victim. You need to let go. We too busy trying to save ourselves. What if I told you that you can save yourself by saving someone else? Then avoid social triggers and environments. Your emotion, boredom, restless, irritable is all a trigger, too. Reminiscing about past, old friends, and environments is number one for drug relapse or recidivism. Remember, same thing, same people, same place, equals same results. Stop living in the past if you are still incarcerated. Let that go, start in the now, be present with a clean slate to reinvest self and peel the new layers off of yourself.

Do not waste a ton of energy and time chasing your tail, burn out and flop down. Riches is not the key to happiness or answers to problem solve. The ego will allow you to believe in bullshit that's not reality, that you can cling on and be attached to falsified concepts. Therefore, be conscious of your time, pick things of value to add, or meaning. You can use this time incarcerated to deflect. You got to be a forward thinker. Our history infinite knowledge and origin like the pyramids. You need to defuse and self-awareness with self-learning to further enable your reform success.

After you discover your superpower niche, use superpower to push super plays and do a super push. The same concept from working from home, except you working from your cell or institution on self and doing creative reform work and implementation. All skills are learnable. Do not allow yourself to be deprived, take action. The ability to set priorities, what's most important and where to put your time. Figure what's your most important, and you will increase your time, income, etc. Do fewer things less important, and do more important things more. Ask yourself if you had 1 hour to get 1 thing you had to get done in 1 day, what will it be? What's the most important thing and can you truly get it done with discipline? Which would be the most valuable thing to accomplish hands down? Do not work in irrelevant things fruitless without payout to outweigh the probative effect or significance. This does not mean a money attachment. Most people have a blind spot and don't want to admit it. Mastering your skill to have and gain confidence.

Big ideas and small turnaround time. Being a big dreamer and stretching yourself to the sky and stars to self-reform incarcerated. Even if you don't have a team or support system, all you need is yourself and to follow your own blueprint steps. Support self, goals, vision, and your craft to reform. Be of service making every day easier for you and your progress. Think of progressive steps ahead to do naturally without asking yourself.

Pushing people to break barriers against the norms and status quo. We as humans are meant to push the needle, evolve, and grow. Just because you don't fit into their box does not mean you're not tangible to your space. It's about not putting people in a box, judgmental, and giving them a space and chance to hear their story, like I did Old Man Duke, bless his soul. To look at in a different lens with a different community and perspective. Provide other fulfilment to people and value, self-awareness. Building processes and helping people structure self to reform is how you help spread and pass on the ILM Blueprint. Your vision needs to be in focus to help people implement strongly or proactively.

It's all Intervention 101. Human beings get into trouble from seeking things versus creating things within self. This is the framework I have structured for you with this ILM Blueprint to elevate and tap into your greatness while discovering your superpowers and creativity. Therefore, you don't have to get bored or in trouble. You can build. Finally, ask yourself to identify all your triggers from emotional to impulses. Is someone pulling on them or you yourself? Is someone playing on them, poking at you, or you are? Be steadfast on self-discipline like a mantra. It's discomfort to change old dynamics, but you must.

The key is having the same vision aligned and connecting to execute and stick to it with others or by self. It's about being able to control your own narrative and establishing your own independence, and lockdown society able to speak up and not let inequality or oppression control incarceration narrative with dehumanization. We able to share our own stories and open up about our struggle. Being a listener and being able to accept feedback or constructive criticism. Pushing past society norms. Make an investment not just in self, but in someone else or people in the pen. ILM helps people see their worth and wake others up, too.

It is always going to be traps, snares, and trouble along the way, but you will find it and with consciousness not getting caught up in your ego. Every practice is discipline. Discipline is good and how we train ourselves to be a new operating system. I am locked up, but I'm free. Physically I am present. You, too, can adopt this method of realization. Remember you must learn to believe against all odds. Establishing a vision and goal, challenge yourself to reform into the new you with a new life and push. Awake and commitment. It spreads through the culture and influences the community and becomes a lifestyle. Follow my ILM Blueprint devoted and sincere to reform, and I will lead you to freedom in all ways mentally, financially, spiritually, and physically. If they wake up, then others around them will wake up and catch it, too. Motivation and enlightenment should come from truth and love. You cannot have unrealistic expectations because stress and hardship will hit while you on your blueprint. It's consistency to your victory with focus. Also you can decriminalize yourself by stop thinking criminal. Stop schemes, plotting, illegal hustling, drug abuse, prostitution, gangbanging, pimpin, and all the above that have criminal ties. No guns either. This all detaches you from criminal activity and crimes to throw you into the biased penal system. This is the true ultimate challenge of letting go to grow. Like I did a 180 turnaround, started hustling all legit, left the gangs, guns, and pimpin alone to evolve into a conscious man. It won't happen overnight, it will happen in steps and commitment. Self-discipline to break patterns and barriers.

A real leader gives direction, problem solves, carves out a clear path, provides transparency and effective solutions. Every leader knows how to think and problem solve. Defining the problems and solutions clearly. Solve problems and solutions with clarity. See yourself as a leader, too. Lead by example and actions. You cannot just merely give directives without implementation. Perform to get results. Leadership is a skill, not a practice. We all have leadership skills naturally in us, not just parenting skillsets. A structure brainstorming session for forwardness. The best solutions are the simplest solutions. Do not be too hard on yourself or others, be careful not to confuse people from being too complex. Make ramifications, decisions that don't slow down your process or progress. What are the decisions you make that impact yourself, family, and goals big? Organization and development structure for your forward growth always.

Lastly, with this ILM Blueprint, I want to address health and leave you some quick health tips. First off, a healthy man has 99 problems, whereas a sick man has one problem. Health consciousness consists of a well-balanced diet and a regular workout routine. Being aware of what you eat and feed your body, especially fast and junk food of high salts and high sugars. Exercise at least 3 to 4 times a week to stay healthy or at least walk every other day. The sole purpose is to keep that blood flow and body vibrations in healthy rotation. All your body functions are based on movement. As humans, we are meant to move around, not lie dormant all day.

Exercise and correct diet helps with spirituality and creativity process. When you walk with a thought bubble or question, your super conscious mind capability kicks in and it helps your brainwave go from beta to an alpha wave. I would do an accountability challenge to self. Every time I would use profanity words, I would do 50 push-ups. I must've done a thousand push-ups the first day. After a while you become conscious of all and words by thinking before you speak or act. For women, you can try this challenge with squats instead of push-ups. This way, you're exercising both your body and mind, which is the greatest power source to develop within.

Mental impact from incarceration has a huge toll on wellbeing and anxiety or depression from being captive and not normal human being habitat, settings, or outdoors versus confined in a cage or a controlled environment with recycled air, not fresh. Mental health well-being and practices to stimulate the senses or mood. With the same daily environment, routine, and people, it creates depression and anxiety at high levels, especially the more toxic environment facilities. They change laws and get a billion dollars in yearly revenue and they don't focus on mental health programs or therapy. Meditation, yoga, and breathing exercises should all be taught and available. However, they don't, but you can push for it at your institution. If not, found your own mental health awareness groups or start with self.

The hacks are meditation, smiling, breathing exercise, mindfulness, and gratitude. Focus on resetting your energy 2 to 3 times a day with refocusing your mind, heart, and breathing to ground and center self. You will find a calmness and your frequency that you vibrate on regardless of what makes you mad, conditions, or environment to thrive and rise above it all. Improve your blood flow, focus all your attention on now, and always bring your attention back to your breathing to stay centered and block everything and everybody else out of your wave aura. Do this as a ritual daily to build into a habit of mental health well-being reset hack to where nothing can penetrate thru to you, or move you and redirect your focal energy point to get beside yourself to make impulsive or bad decisions and relapse off your ILM Blueprint for self-reform. Have boundaries.

Now you have it, the movement, mission, and ILM Blueprint to self-reform thru transformation with education, elevation, self-awareness, innovation, self-discipline, development, and health consciousness core principles. My goal is, again, to leave ILM Blueprint reform for people to adopt at all facilities and continues when I leave, too. It's all to help facilitate and implement change to those who seek betterment that don't know how to. The objective to them to use prison as a platform. Start now and activate. Reverse time they give you and make it work for you versus against you. Give them a stance, voice, and enable them to challenge themselves to self-reform, develop skillsets, mannerisms, spirituality, self-discipline, and tools to be independent. With a better reentry plan into society establishing their independence and relationships successfully. Also can read more of my self-development books to assist more in-depth with skills and principles.

- Chapter 4 -

"BLM & ILM United"

Black Lives Matter and Incarcerated Lives Matter United is the goal and focus point. Unity is one of the main premises for this book. The flipside of the coin is the police not only killing us, including these in custody, lynching-style deaths, they are racial profiling and locking Black men, women, and juveniles up at a 5x ratio more than Whites in rural areas. Therefore, it's 2 main underlying issues, which is number one, they killing us, and number two, they locking us up. This is what I want to get Black Lives Matter attention to and the public as well. They are literally throwing us in a cage or a grave.

To solve any problem, first you have to identify it, then formulate to address it. To fix problematic issues, you must be aware it exists. If you overlook things, they build up and don't go away. This is exactly what happened with the Black Lives Matter movement, that because of these camera phones and body cams, they can no longer ignore that systemic racism and inequality still exist. We can stand up, demonstrate, protest with a loud voice, and stand in arms united.

However, being incarcerated out of sight, out of mind, without phone cams and body cams to see the oppression, abuse, and the systemic racism plagued in the criminal justice system. Those same prejudiced cops with the will to kill Black men, women, and juveniles are trumping up charges, false arrest, and planting guns or drugs on Black men, women, and juveniles, too. We need to be able to hold these same cops accountable for all their biased actions from custody killings to botched targeted arrests that is the leading cause of mass incarceration. Over 1.4 million Black, incarcerated lives. We make up the definition of mass incarceration globally. This mass incarceration needs to end. Emancipation and liberty for all.

While we have the spotlight on racism, social reform justice, unrest, we need to widen that scope and direct that spotlight to shine on ILM, too. That goes hand-in-hand with these vicious systemic racism cop entities. We cannot let them sweep us under the rug fixing other police misconduct issues without arresting and incarceration issues, too. They must be held accountable all across the board. Let's all unite to break their billion-dollar modern-day slave trade oiled massive machine of mass incarceration business and private prison entities.

We are buried alive, no voice, and oblivious to the public, hidden like we don't matter. These 1.4 million Black lives being warehoused in human dog kennels still not free. Look at these numbers alone. If you do not see nothing alarming and problematic. This will have anyone fired up and want to be proactive. From excessive sentence, fees being unpaid, probation violations, drug charges, wrongful convictions, felony murder, partial jury decisions laws, illegal sentences, and reversable court errors, due process violations, and so much more on the extensive list how to railroad a Negro in the criminal justice system.

Integrate both movements, ILM and BLM, and do a united push together on police reform and prison reform. Police misconduct and prosecutor misconduct. Mass incarcerated and police fatality and all systemic racism. Help us push together to break these chains of mass incarceration and injustice. This is how change is made.

My message and mission to Black Lives Matter movement and co-founders or the BLM organizers in each state branch is to first reach out to Incarcerated Lives Matter movement and tap in to the inside. You need people on the inside to tell you the main issues and insight of the strengths, weakness, status, and progress. Set up calls or reach out via email or mail, and please take the initiative to listen and hear these women and inmates' injustices out. I know not everybody is innocent. However, they still all guilty to a corrupt system giving out harsh sentences. Do not let their cries fall on deaf ears. They all victims of their environments and need help to transition for betterment to awake in self-actualization. A lot of us did not have a choice to be born in these projects or hood environment or born Black. This is what we were choosing to go thru in life trials and tribulations to grow from and rise hard like that rose that grew from the concrete. It's currently over a million of incarcerated Black lives stuck in the mud from raw deals without no means, resources, or big billion-dollar organization to help prison reform bills to end mass incarceration to free the modern government slaves as the U.S. Constitution amendment states we are. Slavery is not truly abolished yet. This is another language we have to push to change, too. Law officials, president, etc. vow to do prison reform. Nothing changes.

Black lives matter. If you believe incarcerated lives matter, too, let's unite these 2 movements and push policy reform, and prison reform, mass incarceration, prosecutor misconduct, and police misconduct. Again, throwing us in a grave or a cage, same injustice, same bias inequalities, and the same Black families losing loved ones buried in a grave or cage. Moms cry the same way in grief. A loss is a loss. However, I know the same system, force, and police department entities is response for both sides of the coin that plague Black lives and families, harassing Black communities. The Black man is not an endangered species, just victims since 1619 of racial genocide that still exists. We need to all wake up and unite to crack this whole systemic racism wide open. They pass it down for their generations to implement a modern Willy Lynch Negro blueprint, but we cannot even pull all three generations together to unite to stop it.

We have plenty of intellectuals, professionals, lawyers, lawmakers, and Black people in positions of power. However, it takes one person incarcerated to scream out united, not divided, is how we beat any beast! Everything has a team or consists of massive people operating structure. Unless it's A.I. (artificial intelligence) automated, which a lot of that took teams of 10,000 techs in Silicon Valley to program. Trust me, the systemic racism, they get it and they are all together. Why we cannot even come together, when we have scholars and a Black person in every field on Earth? We all have our superpower, gifts, and specialization position to play piece to this puzzle. We have direction. However, we need direction implementation and to have organized structure, accountability, a spreadsheet plan of action of the reform policies we need to work on in each state. I have been organizing chaos, structure, action plans, advisory boards my whole life. People too busy racing to the top, climbing up the ladder. Sometimes you have to go down the ladder to tell more people at the bottom what's up, meaning every influencer, community leader and organizer/event planner, church leader, athlete, etc., has reach, a following, and respect to be heard. They are the ones to give order, restore order, or implement visions of order. These are the ones you instruct the blueprint and message to get people in ranks and on board to spread the message, movement, and how to push. The street's fathers or O.G.s are all gone, locked up or dead by these same police. We will address this issue further in the book how to tap into the community and building within. It's merely the blind leading the blind out there and the disconnected from the urban community don't know how to stop the record-breaking Black-on-Black killings, or they don't know what to do, the solutions. I do, though.

BLM needs to tap in to the community that has the incarceration high rates to mass incarceration in their personal states. Once they tap into community, they will find leaders and moms tapped into lockdown society. They will lead you to someone on the inside pushing ILM or an injustice with them. You then can help shine a spotlight, stop someone wrongfully convicted on death row from being executed, lead to freedom. We need unity as a whole. We cannot keep standing alone. You all need to be woke to what's going on in the inside by being aligned with someone in the inside in every state along with every state BLM movement chapter. Everyone be accountable for your state prison status and government regulations, funding, programs, sanitation, COVID, etc.

We can defund the police and defund prisons, too. That will really get their attention, too. End mass incarceration by ending these private prisons. Then defunding the state and federal prisons, too. That will decrease a huge percentage of mass incarceration by decreasing the prison population. It's all possible if we united with structure. We can't personally outsource. This is why I am writing this book and started this lockdown society ILM movement to push and be heard loud and clear as a voice to over a million Black incarcerated lives to break through to the ones listening that bought into the incarcerated narratives of us as thugs and criminals, dehumanize us forgotten like we don't have no rights in the U.S. to matter. All to a broken exploited system.

Kim Kardashian, Mya Moore, WNBA star, Common, JayZ, Meek Mill, Yo Gotti, and all reform organizations are woke and can see thru these walls clearly, but none of them can do it alone. We need BLM and ILM movement to focus inwards transparency to push together outwards. It's all over money, they get paid billions to warehouse us literally. Look at it mass productions, no more farms, just massive facilities storing chickens, pigs, cows for more money. This is exactly how they storing us massively, treating us like we animals and branding us to the world as criminals with an Incarcerated Lives Don't Matter tag. It's sad but the real truth. The youth and everyone needs to see this realization. It's nothing the matter with us, it's something the matter with them, which is called hatred and greed. Black people are naturally forgiving and loving people. Don't be blinded by the paradigms they put us in environmental or from drugs. They capitalizing off human storage facilities.

It's definitely time now for BLM and ILM to unite and we all Black lives that matter out there and inside here. Address both issues as a whole. It's essential now that we have their direct attention and tackling the big issue of the elephant in the room. Free my people and stop killing my people on racism, inequality, justice, and reform. Systemic racism within the police department and penal system. Help defund the prisons and free us targeted and arrested by police victims of injustice and hate, too, that fuel the penal criminal justice system. Again, if we push as a whole, we can break thru their system united. They oppress y'all, they oppress us all. Prime real estate investing is prisons with high flip and markup value! It's power in the people and in numbers. Remember, the people is the power.

The public been so disconnected from the prison population, even family is distant now. Lack of support and outside structure is what the prison corporations want for higher recidivism rates. This is why they do not fund a lot of real skilled prison programs, education, or rehabilitation. They want the public to stay their distance so they don't dismantle their sweet billion-dollar Negro warehouse business or pry in their real criminal enterprise money laundering taxpayers' funds for personal gains and growth hockey stick projected funding. They schemes we need to track and trace the real data, not the made-up paperwork or paid-off directors of prisons, wardens and shareholders of private prisons. We need accounts audited and investigation going back for generations to see their same old behavior entity patterns of money garnishing. Judges and prosecutors, too.

It needs to be an alliance with BLM and ILM. The movements need to be aligned. All BLM organizers in all cities need to not be afraid to take the initiative to reach out and connect to open up lines of ample communication and awareness on the inside to help be our voices of injustices, end mass incarceration, and pushing prison reform.

My push is not your push, however. My push should be your push because we as colored people are all indirectly infected. Humanity is the essential key, even if you do not have a bone of empathy for incarcerated lives or feel like we matter, we still human. Do a push for humanity.

ILM have so much on their hearts, once you see them as people, not criminal titles. They have fear, hope, love like all human traits, too. It takes real humanity. These people are trying to reach out, express their broken stories and injustices. They have such values and newfound values.

Being incarcerated and lockdown society always been the original cancelled culture before 2020 cancel cultures trending norms. Then people always hashtag or talking about free this and free that. However, their actions and push don't match their tweets or voices at all. They simply want to be seen, but they defend the ILM unseen. Nor is ILM seen by them, either.

BLM and ILM movements united, we can push so much more like the Belgian horses can pull so much more weight together. Let me share this metaphor and break down the Belgian French horses. They pull a total of 8,000 lbs. apiece solo. However, together they can pull 19,000 lbs., and if you train and push them, 2 can pull a total of 25,000 lbs., facts. There, imagine what we can do by a united push best of both societies. Take actions big and small. When we together, play together, pray together, vibe together, and sing its harmony. It sounds and looks good, plus it's very catchy for others to adopt or plant a mustard seed. Remember, you don't have to immediately know the how. The how will show up on the commitment to what you want and why, plus focus energy, too.

Being incarcerated, your stance is different with vigor or empowered. You have a structural power stride, strut, or walk. Head up, never letting your chin touch your chest. All body empowerment glowing. By putting your body into a more powerful position or power poses, you change your physiology. Therefore, if we move as a whole body of power of people, we can attack and bring down other bodies and entities. Is you all with it and riding beside us ILM, like Drake? Let's push with unity!

Finally, they say do not have regrets in life, that's cliché. I do not believe that unless you privileged. I've plenty of regrets on bad, wrong, or impulsive decisions I made in life, including being incarcerated from my kids and loved ones. Even though I found myself incarcerated like Stanley Tookie Williams and started writing education and kids' books or Malcolm X did with spirituality, and Mandela freedom fighter, and push for incarceration education. I'm not about regret not lifting my pen to use my superpower as a megaphone to raise my voice to connect and merge these 2 movements to unite. Now you got the inside attention and outside attention to push as a whole woke force to deal with. It's truly beautiful to display, organize with structure and see the perpetual progress being hammered to reform and get people home.

- Chapter 5 -

"Police & Police Reform"

With all the social unrest and protests going on out there after the George Floyd, Ahmaud Arbery, and Breonna Taylor from lethal force and racism ignited the push on top of this COVID pandemic.

Police misconduct and prosecutor misconduct. Them same biased police officers in the systemic racism play a part of arresting us on bogus, trumped-up, or falsified charges. A lot of wrongful arrests lead to wrongful convictions of people of color.

When they see us, the Central Park 5 wrongfully accused and convicted in the racist justice system. Jim Crowism over divide and apartheid. The racial narrative to justify lynching Blacks after slavery crimes against Blacks and summons the people in public to come watch the hanging of the Negros with their families, too. A lot of police hiring is autonomous and you need a high school diploma, emotional and psych evaluation.

It's difficult to police the bad seeds in the criminal justice system web. We need more defense attorneys and judges from within that's of color non-biased, fair and impartial. We want and demand change reform on both sides, including the inside. We just see the same storyline. The world forgot about us incarcerate due to this same inequality chain and police systemic racism. A system that makes government slaves, servitude out of people, including extended probation, you free with an invisible chain around your neck, too.

They help family and society keep that narrative of we all belong to be incarcerated and deserve it. The incarcerated stories that get erased and name, productivity, push unknown. The priors, crimes while on papers, relapsing and repeated offenders from not having proper tools, skills, mentors, and equality in society to produce jobs, income, and success.

We stuck in this jail paradigm that all mass incarceration and lockdown society are criminals and deserve stiff harsh sentences or pieces of trash. All outcasted and banished or exiled from society without real due process, justice and bias. I will never give up on the million Black men and women nor juveniles lost and oppressed in the system. I'll help heal and rebuild them to self-reform while further awakening and enlightening them. Again, this why I founded this ILM movement in 2017 and formulated the reform blueprint principles to implement.

Judicial and prison reform, economic oppression, inequality, systemic racism, racial profiling, police brutality/misconduct, and exerted charges, with highest charges possible. Racial disparity. Police characterize people of color, especially Black men, a threat and jury guilty from being in custody.

Biased jury pools for people of color and have 98 percent conviction rate, especially all dangerous crimes over non-dangerous. Just imagine if you can wear makeup on trial as a White person. Would you be convicted then? Hell no, acquitted and the mass incarcerated rate will be cut in a huge margin. Including partial jury pool 10 to 2 convictions, not unanimous.

Mass incarceration is also due to the war on drugs, and most convictions are drug-related, therefore, most arrests are drug-related, too. Julius Jones in OKC currently on death row still and has evidence to present his innocence. He also had a tainted jury pool with racial slurs and got wrongfully convicted. These tainted biased racial jury pools need to be stopped and more diversified. Systemic racism lies in their ranks, too. This is why the criminal justice system and whole ethics need to be dismantled and rebuilt or reprogrammed with data reporting metrics of every case due process and outcome. The juror stated in the deliberation room they should take that N-word out back and shoot him. Julius Jones' alleged crime was against the killing and carjacking of a White man.

Cameron Boyd, a K.C. Black man, got shot and killed in his driveway by police, and the cops planted a gun on him, too. C-Murder, aka Corey Miller, Master P's brother, still incarcerated almost 20 years later on a Louisiana partial jury verdict. Malcom Pens and his brother locked up and convicted of murder, a crime they didn't do, too, in Tulsa, Oklahoma. Danny Robinson, Jr., Marcques Hill, and Parish Swift innocent in Nebraska and Big Burdean in the feds.

Over 65 percent Black men wrongful convictions overturn, which equals over 6,000 years served that young, Black men cannot get back. They working on 145 wrongful conviction cases, and Black is only 7 percent of that. The data there 1 out 4 Black men gets locked up, 5x times more likely than White men. White privilege people and rich people get slaps on the wrist for same crimes Black people get excessive sentences for. A present bias.

It's typically 200 to 300 assigned for legal counsel by the state to one public defender. They pretenders to help and care about you as their client. The system pays them for closing your case and getting you to sign a deal and plea bargain out. The system is the beast, and they feed it by selling you out at trial ineffective assistance of counsel. This system is broken in these are all the internal components you cannot see from the outside that needs real reform. Also the cause of mass incarceration. From prosecutor misconduct to police misconduct, all germinate growth of mass incarceration bubble and driving by greed and racism. That bubble is what we all need to focus on to burst united together. We can one day have a prison reform breakthrough, free of chains and out those boxes.

We need to think bigger and focus on breaking the main reform issues with proactive plans of actions. I am giving the outside an exclusive look into mass incarceration with a mass scope directly. All the ongoing injustices, bias, and penal systemic racism that America needs to wake up and clear their eyes to modern slavery still exists and they are getting rich and needs to be defunded and stopped.

It's vessels from dominance, slavery, police brutality, and mass incarceration. It's all one cipher and connected from the judges, lawyers, cops, prosecutors, district attorneys, private prisons, stocks, private vendors, and prison healthcare organizations. We must petition to put up bills for Congress to rewrite that U.S. Constitution amendment that enslaved mass incarceration. It needs to be knocked down and subtracted like a Confederate statue. If we aim right, we can knock that capitalism crown down and help end mass incarceration. Remember, the Constitution was written while we were still slaves as Afro-American Black folks.

The fear is the capital system they built for generational wealth will be compromised or stolen their cash cows. I want you all to realize factual, it is about money and a real profitable business. It's not a nonprofit entity. You cannot Google who got rich or wealthy off prison entities, healthcare, stocks, or commodities. You may see and find celebrities that pop up like Jordan putting $40 million into private prisons, or MC Hammer buys Oakland police cruisers and helicopter. However, you won't find none of these other mass incarceration wealthy exploiters and their families on Google. You can find anything else on Google, but this hidden info and data for a reason. People who can see what others cannot see are the ones who are able to break thru and move or shift the world. Again, I've a vision a hundred years from now, it will be frowned upon like slavery. It starts today, now, on our timeline with our united push.

They do not put money into social, psychiatric, mental health, or drug and educational programs. We need prison reform on the inside and cash bail reform. Also that incarceration cures all solutions to courts, puts you in jail over fines, child support, etc. Everybody in is not thugs, and fees can be resolved in other ways, like community service.

Recently, 87 people were arrested during protests, and protestors getting incarcerated with ramped-up charges is a prime example. Charged with felony, which is definitely ramped-up for protesting or demonstrating. This is tone-deaf and prime example lack of justice for Breonna Taylor that they were protesting for.

Trump urging governors to use military and inciting violence via tweets during the pandemic and sparking further racial divide and split in the country. He is incompetent to run the country and unethical. He lies constantly and is a narcissist. We cannot defund Trump, but we can dethrone him and vote him out of office ASAP! He failed on prison reform, the pandemic, mandating COVID masks, social justice, police reform, and a list of so much more to back up facts.

The police unions, they throw away misconduct reports after 4 to 5 years or do not actually file the misconduct reports that the citizens file their complaints to be logged. Therefore, we cannot track the data to pinpoint these cops of behavior patterns of misconduct and prejudice. It's definitely radicalism in their ranks. A gang, not a brotherhood, with a license to kill Negros at will. Even their police chief stays silent to the race matters and department records of violations and misconduct. This needs police reform for behavior action accountability to get these same cops off the streets who are racial profiling, target arresting, and killing Black men, women and children. Need to be able to pull up all their records of citations, complaints, and disciplinary actions.

With race matters and police reform, it should be an independent database for all arrest history and police misconduct for the public to catch any red flags or patterns of behavior and racial bias. Mandatory body cams, if they do not have body cams on during an incident or deliberately turn them off, they should immediately be terminated from the force. All outside investigation and independently beside the Department of Justice for indie autopsies for police homicides. Banning all excessive force tactics, chokeholds, and restraints. Also, policy changes, deescalation, behavior strategies training. Fear tactics abolished, bestow plural officer accountability. No officers being disciplined after flagrant misconduct cases, public or non-public spotlight. All Black cop turncoats need a new job and a wake-up reality check.

There is an imminent rush and push to unite to get Trump out of office. We need everybody to get out and vote. Mask up and get to them polls, lines, and be patient. He already attempting to defund the postal services to make executive orders so he can dictate the mail-in votes. We need intervention to counter that by showing up in world record turnouts of all Colored and White people of all ages, including all the felons that can still vote in your state or had their rights to vote restored. I wish people incarcerated vote count and could actually vote, because over a million of us would have really made a difference regardless not being a delegate. In Florida the felons need their restitutions and fees paid to vote first. This is where we need to have organizations and influencers step in and help fund to pay off debt to get those 5 percent votes, too. I did see some NBA players step up to help pay some fines and designing BLM merch to fundraise.

It's been voter fraud and voter suppression in 2020 elections all over, but mainly in the rural Black communities. The machines too slow, old, or broke, and they make people stand outside 8 hours to discourage people from voting with antics. We must continue to push strong like our ancestors did. Trump is really filing executive orders trying to hijack the mail-in votes, seriously. Let's wake up, people, and unite. They are not playing, so why should we?

You must remember how these judges also play a huge key role and banish Black lives into mass incarceration abuse of discretion and abuse of power, including bias misconduct. It's racist judges, too. Some reports show judges being alcoholics and drinking every morning before court sessions. These are the ones we need to weave out the criminal justice system because they are the main keyholders with the power to hand down the sentences, concurrent or consecutive, excessive, or even dismissals and reversals. Again, the reason why they do not overturn a lot of cases with burden of proof evidence or ample significant newly discovered or withheld evidence is because the risk of being retroactive reversals. Like if they let one person go based on a clerical error, they would have to let a hundred thousand others go on the same fundamental error, too. Therefore, the judge would rather deny you even if all in your favor. Regardless if you have a million-dollar lawyer or appellate lawyer, you and your family still don't have nothing coming or due process and fair justice.

I know all this is from personal experience with my cases state and federal law. Also hundreds of others I aid and assist with legal work and appeals. You cannot win once you get within its concrete quicksand, stuck and buried alive. 90 percent of people in here tell me they wish they did not go to trial and should've took that hard plea bargain deal. Even my appeal process was an emotional headache and years of waiting, including doing dead time stuck on pause in a limbo. I was walking what we call on the compound bowlegged, aka doing consecutive sentences and time back to back. All my hard work and lawsuits got all denials, even with hired legal counsels. Nothing but hard headaches and gray areas of legal loopholes they throw you into. This is why we need to unite to formulate and break this already broken system plagued with systemic racism and oppression. I'm letting you know not to drive my point home or across, but to point out all the pain points that you all did not know clearly exist without being able to experience it. I'm telling you all how to come together to tackle this beast because you cannot tame it, and I'm speaking from the belly of this beast like Jonah.

Therefore, really look at this in scope open-minded. Why after reversible errors, innocent, affidavits, recant statements, judges still using their own discretion and bias? Let's focus hard on these judges and their pattern of bias and defund these judges, too. From the prosecutors misconduct to the detectives coercing witnesses and collaborating their stories to identify people wrongfully accused like the Central Park 5 really still exist Monday thru Friday in courtrooms all throughout the nation. We still can't see it, though, and know how to fix it with everyone worried about self and disorganized.

We have to really adamantly be willing to engineer our own core clauses to end mass incarceration. Identify the pain points like I have mentioned and pointed out to you throughout this book and have a quest or mission to solve it. Together, not solo, put the people in the position of power or their superpower niche field to do what they excel in well.

Number one way to defund the prisons to end mass incarceration is to cut the cost of incarceration. The private prisons will not bear the cost of incarceration because they simply get paid to house cons at their human storage facilities. Whereas, to bear the cost of incarceration means to pay for each person's imprisonment. They get on average $75K federal to house inmates, and $50K state average per inmate. We need to cut that cost. Especially jails are not seeing none of the used taxpayers' money into these inside programs or rehabilitations. This is called hush money in their personal pocket.

How to knock down a building, you need to look at the frame and how it's structured to destruct or explode. We cannot do a demolition without stripping things on inside first. Tackle the beast inside out and dismantle it.

Have petitions signed to get on ballot of your state. Private prisons do contracts to state. We need to get the states to stop contracting out to private prisons or private vendors and private healthcare that they have their hands and stocks all into, too. This is what all the defund the prison focal points are and aim to target first. Then, we will start to take a dent out of mass incarceration. Even celebrities funding private prisons need to stop investing in human trafficking slave trading entities. Stop listening to their financial advisors or investors about private prisons or vendors long-term investing.

To these private health organizations to the prisons and vendors or prison manufacturers for supplies and commissary like the Keefes and Bob Barkers need to all be defunded by cutting the contracts. Suspend their private contracts and take away all their contract resources. These private vendors that sell commodities to the prison chains also tax and exploit the inmate population with markup price items triple times to the Walmart value. Or they simply have it manufactured specifically for prison use and sale only. It's all connected hand-in-hand. Everyone has a piece of this sweet mass incarceration pie. We need to unite and push to defund the prisons and police entities, which is how to reform the police and prisons using all these methods and focal targeted points mentioned. Justice is for the rich and privileged, not us Black or Hispanic minorities. Mothers of slain victims from police misconduct and mothers of incarcerated Black men, women, and juveniles to the penal system all still haven't had no justice for their loved ones being true victims of hate crimes and systemic racism. Let's come as one voice to push reform for all. Your battle is my battle. Their battle is our true battle, too. It's no indifference, just one cause and one push for all. One fight for all. We all fighting for the same storyline and theme reform, equality, and justice while rewriting the Constitution to end mass incarceration.

Have you ever noticed that people on death row sit 20-plus years waiting to be executed and wondered why? This is not because of legal stays or appeal exhaustion time, because people who waive all their appeal rights or innocent people fighting against their wrongful execution. It's merely because of revenue, once again the price they get per year per imprisonment. Adding to the yearly billion-dollar streaming revenue. Now if you defund their death penalty drugs, that will get their attention, too.

We need to take action. Throwing Hispanic kids in cases separated from families. The DACA Act Obama put into effect to prove that and people working in the U.S. for citizenship. Trump vetoed and threw out, which left people, kids, and families in border cages. They are working to reform it temporarily. This is why we all need to come together, Blacks, Hispanics, and other minorities to push for equality, reform, and Trump out of office immediately on top of COVID pandemic.

Finally, on police reform, they have a Brady's list to track law enforcement officials with integrity concerns. However, it's no real officer accountability. They bounce from department to department, no losing badge or license. They lie, and prosecutor doesn't pursue them or prosecute them. They can even retaliate against whistleblowers. They published a searchable database. However, it's inaccurate. We need to make and reform a real foolproof one, together.

- Chapter 6 -

"COVID Pandemic"

In this chapter I want to address the COVID-19 pandemic in the prisons and county jail or federal holding facilities. Also the effects of it in the criminal justice system, plus my direct personal experience inside.

As of August 2020 right now as I write this book, the number of incarcerated COVID-19 deaths is 1,200. Yes, it hit its thousand mark. However, this is if the reported data is correct. Some facilities only report COVID-19 death if the autopsy states that's the reason of death. Therefore, it can be upwards in the 2,000 to 3,000 range, possible.

We are on the brink of flu season, too. Being incarcerated in close quarters is a microcosm to spread viruses fast. Once someone gets sick, everyone gets sick. It's all recycled air, not fresh air. Only time to get fresh air incarcerated is when you go outside, which movement is limited and has time restrictions, especially the higher custody level yard you're on. I am classified with high risk points to a level 5 supermax yard, which is considered a lockdown yard. Therefore, with us not being able to move, we're glued like sitting ducks. It's currently 534 inmates and 236 staff members that tested positive for COVID-19 in this AZDOC Florence, Eyman complex prison where I am still being housed at right now.

The main underlying issue is being incarcerated, you absolutely cannot social distance. It's impossible. The inmates that have flu-like symptoms, they isolate them into one COVID-19 wing with others showing symptoms, too or actually positive with COVID-19. This causes panic because the ones that do feel a little symptoms do not want to go to the infected COVID-19 isolation wings to catch it for sure, or not to die alone without help on a cold slab and cannot breathe. In jail it's no respirators by the dozen available. At this unit it's currently 2 of them. Let alone bed space to isolate every inmate. Therefore the spread is inevitable, and you have staff and kitchen staff not wearing masks bringing it in to the institutions, spreading it to inmates. Spitting, chewing tobacco, or tossing cigarette butts everywhere, too.

The worst cases get transferred to an outside local hospital. However, even the hospital bed spaces are limited because they will use that bed space for the public first before an inmate. This makes us see we don't matter incarcerated, especially to the public.

I am asthmatic, too. I'd rather take my chances at life on a ventilator than nothing. I know that's last resort efforts, but it's better than nothing. They don't have the proper chemicals to clean surfaces, especially disinfect that the CDC recommended in here. We have to use shampoo and bodywash jailhouse cleaning concoctions to be proactive in prevention with what we have within grasps. If you shaking your head, wow, imagine how we feel and pain inside.

Next, they finally gave us 2 COVID-19 masks made out of prison boxers cotton material. Before that, we were using socks and shirts wrapped up like an orange ninja. It's not as effective like an N-95 medical mask, but it's better than being naked and exposed. Their mask is a joke. My sock works better. Again, they don't care. We do not matter to them. The strong ones make it, and the ones with underlying health conditions do not stand a fighting chance.

Then, we started to get a few off-brand cleaning solutions and bars of state soap, but the incarcerated COVID rates continue to be problematic, increasing, adding to the crisis. As for the inmates that seek help and want dire need of medical attention, the prisons refuse to give them temperature checks or medical assistance. They tell the inmates if you talking, you are breathing and standing, that you are fine. Basically you have to literally fall out to get help and medical care. For many, that's too late already. You can't wash hands properly, either.

This is the same problem in county jails or federal holding facilities bandwidth. They cannot contain it or take care of all the COVID inmates properly. We need real COVID masks and real chemicals to reduce the spread. However, these prisons do not tap into the state or government funds, claiming they are over budget.

It also has caused a slowdown in criminal justice system and courts for due process, jurors, bonds, transfers, rulings, hearings, arraignments, and trials. Because of my chronic asthma condition, I am high risk for COVID-19 where it attacks as pulmonary virus. Therefore, me and others with higher risk health chronic conditions qualify for a compassionate release. The same type of relief they have been letting celebrities out of jail on per COVID pandemic to do the remainder of their time out on house arrest or home confinement.

I put one in to the state. It was denied based on them saying I had to address the director of the prisons, which the AZDOC director David Shinn's office responded and denied me. I submitted a second motion for reconsider compassionate release, which got denied again. AZDOC per Governor Doug Ducey is not granting no prisoners compassionate release due to COVID pandemic. He stated this live on a newscast, too. This is the same governor that denied my book publications and practice once I appealed it from AZDOC banning me. I also did several other inmates' compassionate release motions in different AZ counties. This is why I say mass incarceration is a big business and an unofficial Fortune 500 company, which is a huge humanitarian issue from health risk and fatal harm's way.

This is fear being enclosed and isolated during COVID sickness without family members being able to see you or lose you. Especially if you less than a year to your release date. They have been putting a petition in for the feds to release inmates non-dangerous within a year left, which is good because I love people with passion for reform of criminal justice system. Treatment is needed, not prison. Environment programs are needed to focus on treatment. Deflection, addiction treatment. Now we can track the data, share it transparency to focus and have successful prison and policy reform. With these recent months and spotlight, the data is driven more on reform to use the numbers to change it.

All the high stress levels in lockdown society due to COVID pandemic is a very intense environment each day of uncertainty and doing your best to stay safe. A lot of inmates feel like we don't stand a chance or matter to the world. I push as much positive energy and vibrations to keep those around me strong, in faith, and with positive energy.

I would like to share a few other matter-related stories with you. Do not get it confused. This is not about the victim mentality. This is about the psychological effect of society's don't-matter narrative that footprints on your mental, especially being of color since day one in America, including society actions on us, too. Can you uplift over a million Black men, women, and juveniles with confidence to know they too matter, even though they are currently incarcerated and made some mistakes? No excuses, however. They are worthy of another chance and human, too. Nobody is perfect. They are either influenced from drugs or their dysfunctional environments just like I, too, was before my true discovery of self-identity. Everyone in life has a chance to truly find one's self, your passions, gifts, and life mission. Time, dedication, and self-awareness.

Back in New York City in the '90s, it was a store called PathMart, where you can walk up to the back of the clerk ringing up the grocery items and bag the shoppers' groceries and take them outside to load into people's cars for tips. I was young and trying to make a few dollars. I carried an Italian lady's groceries after I bagged them up to her car and loaded them. Afterward I stood there looking at her like she owes me something. She perked her nose up in the air, then told me why am I looking for a tip? She is not paying me for helping her out when I should've been in school. I frowned at her and told her I will never help her ass again. She spit at me and hopped into her sedan, locking the doors. She sped off out of PathMart parking lot, making a younger version of myself feel unappreciated and like as a young Black teen I didn't matter.

This was the same exact day I was in Manhattan working with my dad at his job with a company called DreamHire that rented out live instruments to bars, clubs, entities, or celebrities. We were on our way to Eddie Murphy's spot in Jersey when we ran into JayZ. My dad told him, "This is my son," proudly. I remember seeing JayZ solo with so much vibrant energy to himself. It was not cocky or confidence. He had an energy of aura like he knew he mattered, no matter what others thought. Plus he was moving thru Manhattan by himself like it was a hundred of him. It was Jay's presence that was so strong that made me see what self-worth was. Long as you see and know you matter, who cares what the world thinks of you? Even my dad trying to boast of me being his son did not boost me with surety like Jay-Z did. It's all a true story and feelings of the '90s.

Another person with incredible aura of energy was DMX. He has an innate sixth sense and can see out of his third eye. Despite DMX's drug abuse he battles, he's one of the realest, whether you like his brutal honesty or not. I was locked up with DMX back in the 4th Ave. Maricopa County Jail in Phoenix. I was still using a wheelchair to go to court because my leg and hardware of metal rods and screws was still fresh. I was not supposed to put a lot of weight on it for 6 months. I was standing up, stretching my leg. I looked up and X was right there in shackles and cuffs, looking at me. He asked me, Am I good? Also, what they talking about? I told him 12 years. X shook his head and told me I am meant for something great and special. That either way, I could walk down whatever the judge gave me. I told X I can barely walk to court, and we both laughed. Me and X were housed in the same pod for a while before they moved him. He would have his pastor come see him a lot and was connected spiritually to God and the universe, too. Later I found out my GMa Lawson, whose maiden name is Holloway, is related to DMX's Grandma Holloway, too, that passed away. The Holloways in New York are all related. However, my whole point of this story is no matter how the world turns their backs on DMX, he made me feel like I mattered, too, and treated me like I was family before I found out we had family ties.

Now, we know that power corrupts and being incarcerated during a COVID pandemic while confronting White supremacy facing all angles of an inch of breakthrough and prosperity of relief we seek. It's still challenging and an uphill battle of faith, endurance, and strength. Where most gave up on hope, themselves, and the outside world. They simply feel defeated, like they truly don't matter and it's detrimental. Therefore, I would like to share a few more breaking points that helped me feel like I did matter and can break through against all odds especially being incarcerated.

I was in the hole lockdown when a Black property sergeant kicked his boot at the bottom of the door and said, "Wake up, pimpin, I got your book manuscripts." Then he popped my door open. I told him, "Do I have to sign a contraband form to send the manuscript out?" He told me no. That he came down here to personally hand me my manuscript I sent out and paid to get it typed up. Also he was surprised that I was writing and self-publishing my books from in jail and doing something with my time. It was urban novel *Pimp of Da Ratchetts Part II, Vegas Edition*. He wanted me to be able to proofread it and see my reward of progress and fruits of labor. He also let me know I was thinking outside the box and was destined to get somewhere great in life, too, which made me feel like I matter. That property sergeant came to me like a messenger God sent at my lowest point after they banned me from self-publishing incarcerated and my independent Chop-A-Style Publishing Company. I never gave up on writing, he just gave me the encouraging words I needed to hear at the right time to push 10x harder. After this I stepped my writing up, which as you see resulted in that 46-plus number. It was unexplainable the energy and innate peak flow it spiraled inside my shift of brainpower. It's like some of the greats say, they do not know how they do it, they just do it.

Lastly, this prison librarian named Mr. Parker believed in me with no doubt and would help me with copies and notaries. Plus I would share ideas with him, especially on print on demand and my self-publishing from the prisons and reform blueprint visions. Parker used to do Secret Service training and had his own security company for years. We would share stories, but he recognized real, it was not just from seeing all the tattoos over my face and canvas. He clearly could tell I'd been thru a lot and had an unfair hand dealt in life, and a rough life with still a bright personality. Parker also saw all the penal oppression I suffered from trying to rise and do something from my heart legit. He saw my struggles, obstacles, and shut down barriers, and me still pushing despite the impossible with little or no outside resources. He knew I would break through one day and told me when I get my books and publishing company off the ground self-publishing, he would have them right there in the prison library for others incarcerated to read and build. He was not just being merely generous, Parker actually believing me without a doubt. Genuine. He was a redhead White man that treated me like I was a human being and matter. Despite my two color barriers being Black and being in orange prison attire. That gave me healing energy to push, that I matter, and all is possible. It's rare someone working inside an institution sees you for you, because they really see right thru and past you. They only see an inmate number as they check you off on their count sheets timely.

For the lifers in lockdown society, you matter, too. You all can find self and do projects and find skillset in your reform process, too. You can live your best life even though you do not have an actual release date. You can pay it forward, tell your story and help mentor others and be youth advocates for new younger people and teens entering lockdown society with no guidance. You can join the ILM movement and spread awareness, connect with some outside, reform and youth organizations to be a spokesperson influencer. Or anything you want to do, because it's not over for you because you are incarcerated. Remember, long as your heart still beating and you still breathing, it's never too late. You really matter and have a place and purpose and life. It's all highly possible to connect and reach out far as your visions take you to, without these never-coming-home narratives that chain your mind or growth down. You guys are the gatekeepers of lockdown society for the youth.

Finally, during this COVID pandemic and outbreak in the penal jail system, I want to thank JayZ, Meek Mill, Yo Gotti, and Reform Alliance, plus other organizations donating COVID masks to the prisons.

- Chapter 7 -

"Influencers Tap In"

"Y'all surprise Tekashi told...real niggas never fold..."—Nipsey Hussle the Great

Nipsey Hussle got it and had the blueprint to it and so loved by all the realness. He already was tapped in to the pen and knew incarcerated lives matter. Nip also knew and saw the value of reform and love of each one teach one principle. Nipsey didn't believe in preaching, only by your actions while being in silence versus trying to do things just to be seen. Nipsey Hussle died helping someone fresh out of incarceration reintegrating into society. He was about community building and investing in the community. Giving kids, homeless people, and ex-cons a chance that they normally would not have in the urban environments. Make sure you all read my Nipsey Hussle lockdown society dedication tribute book, too. It's some of the realest words I ever wrote from the heart because he taught and showed us so much and represented us. Most of all that incarcerated lives matter, too. He really believed in his heart and led by his actions for example. Rest in peace, Nip!

Influencers tap-tap-tap in to the pen and community like Nipsey did, too. Show face, use platforms to lead by example and show up invested in community. Be able to come to the hoods, share love, knowledge, and spread awareness with your influence. Invest in the people. We all being called upon right now. They want us to stay sleep while they out building generational wealth for theirs. Bring the hood and Blacks back together. Now it's time to open eyes to stop killing and fighting invisible enemy of self. Influencers and organizations Black-owned help us before putting your energy, time, and money into someone else. With all this mass incarceration and police killings of Blacks being the new norm, we need united support with the people of influence and community leaders in here and out there, too. Help heal, invest, and restore order and action.

Everybody talks about the well without tapping into that well, go to the direct source. Black Lives Matter, organizations, prison reform advocates, law reform programs all tap in to the Black men and women that's pushing in lockdown society. They will give you real data and direct source or solutions. Even the environment temperatures, conditions, buzz, or current injustices the public needs to know about or assist on.

Please know and remember in lockdown society, it's hidden jewels inside. It's up to you to start digging and spreading people to dig and invest. Help us change the narrative, transfer from a negative to a positive and productivity. The incarceration population needs a real chance at reform and influencers, outside connections, and resources help people to see and seek transformation and change. I cannot do it by myself. I can write the reform blueprints. However, some still need help, push, and therapy to implement. Also sponsorship programs in place or sponsoring people incarcerated or our ILM movement to get books, programs, and speakers inside the facilities.

I encourage and challenge you all, not just influencers, to dive into these hidden jewels of mass incarceration. If you have brothers, uncles, cousins, sons, and daughters incarcerated, reach out to them, see how they doing or what they doing with their time. Offer your support, send them books or the education building they need. You do not have to send money all the time. It's more about your love, support, and making a connection. People incarcerated want to feel like they matter. With just that little sense of worth and feeling, it pushes them a long way, makes better days, too. Even a simple letter and health and welfare check on them goes a long way and great for their mental health in these intense toxic environments and conditions. Especially if you are mad at them or were mad at them for getting into trouble or drugs leading up to their jail time. Now is the time to break through to them with a clear mind and sit them down. They not too busy or distracted like the outside world. Do not simply give up on your loved ones in these crisis times of pandemic and unrest. It's time to heal, amend, and tap back in to the pen.

Tap in to ILM movement influencers, celebrities, and all organizations help support and invest into mass incarceration with jobs, reentry programs, housing, and mental health, too. Give jobs, products, provide more resources to help inside reform and rebuild. Put your money into not just investing self but to investing others. Good deeds are priceless and more impressionable in life. Especially if you're blessed with a higher position, wealth, and knowledge. Having a dream job that you always wished is different from having a solid heart to help people with no means rehabilitate. It's not always black and white. The gray areas in the mass incarceration space needs to be exposed. The reason is to do what is right for people and humanity. I want to bridge this gap that is so clear that everyone deserves help, a second chance and guidance that's lost. We need to wake the people up to the grand scheme behind the scenes of mass incarceration billion-dollar entities.

We ourselves can help stop or prevent people from coming to jail by reforming actions and lifestyles. By tapping in, you would see all the systemic issues, troubleshoot areas inside these 4 walls. Then exactly where you can show support and can contribute to. In here people are mostly rejected from deals, contracts, or selling their creative crafts and artwork. Or like rejects flat out. Do not get me wrong. I don't want you looking at it as an emotional investment. I want you to look at it from your heart space to help versus gain. Also to have a better tool belt and advocate for an ally to the mass incarceration and ILM community. To learn and understand the connection to the inside to build new bridges. Whether you're a visionary, organizer, religious supporter, speaker, coach, etc., you still can reach out and touch some spirit that's broken within. You have to be clear of the worth of people in numbers. People is power. They give you back what you teach them. Share your love, reach, and support.

Pastors and church groups along with Imams come into the facilities often, devote time, energy, and support. They make connections and provide relief, mental and spiritual. People locked up don't feel like others respect them. Therefore they are afraid to reach out, open up, and reflect how they can change their life. Some people actually try to get help and get boundaries put up or doors slammed shut in their faces. Society places us in this raw rejecting space and narratives we unworthy and undeserving of opportunities. This is the environment where society mentally removes us from any endeavors and revelations to be reborn. People tell their stories because they want to be free and free themselves. You have freed yourself, had help, mentors, therapy, influence, and even wrote essays to express yourself and communicate to be heard.

People in lockdown society can't get heard. Especially men that can't show their feelings because of masculinity culture that from being oppressed creates radicalism to lash out, being so angry to explode on others versus being defused to not be reacted off emotional triggers. This is how I get a lot of people to reform, offering them a place and space to share. Like write down past hurts, wrongs, and future plans. Or self-talk and affirmations to help get it out and heard to rewire their brains after you heal. We can eradicate all this darkness and toxic environments or masculinity. We need to be in for that fight, show up for that march, support, cause, and you will feel great. Lead you down a whole different path. Showing up for different people and a little way goes a long way and helps you unlock different chambers of your heart and energy. Let's have perspective questions and dive deeper by tapping in to ILM in depth. You all have a privilege of exposure to push it.

This system of oppression of Black men and women incarcerated created not just generation barriers, socialism, and microcosms that permeate mental enslavement. You do not understand the barriers on top of being people of color being incarcerated to get investment, support, funding, and job skills. The impact on our kids' kids from us not being supported because of these barriers. Look for community, future, mass incarceration investing. We have to have a rational overall uplifting helpful perspective to others and shift. I think when it's people that don't owe you does kindness to add value. Help us engage and take mass incarceration into a bigger space to get bigger results for reform. To look at systems, justices, and creative framework. I have created a platform and opportunity to be a mirror and voice to people or mass incarceration to stand up, speak up and help reform out the realness of my heart. Therefore I need to outsource to the public and influencers and people of all to tap in to help us transform, reform, and betterment.

My mission was to create a library, write personal development books to help ILM reform and skillsets upon reentry. Then create an easy-to-implement blueprint for self-reform. My funding issues were getting all these books produced, then into these prisons. Plus help Black women incarcerated with woman leadership. However, I could not afford for all my books to get edited even at a discounted rate. This also where we need assistance, not just money, if you can contribute skillsets, tips, and consultants. We have artists to do cover design, freelance writers for copy, content, and creative writing. Script writers, ghost writers, musical creative writers, too. I have almost 30 authors lined up to produce under my ILM Chop-A-Style library. I will use an each-one-help-fund-one method, where we put a percentage of each book back into the pot to pay it forward to produce the next incarcerated author book project with an automated process for all the writers reforming to be heard, too, while showcasing their talents.

This is why we need the public to invest and tap in to provide incarcerated people with equal chances to build, set up skillsets, have reentry valid plans and revenue, and acquire proper housing. Help establish independence. When people get out with skillsets, trades, or employment, they are 10x more likely to be successful upon reentry versus relapse or recidivism. This is also why I do encourage and challenge society's influencers, organizations, and people of interest to give a real valid chance, employment, contracts, deals, etc. to mass incarceration. Enable them to be able to reform and reentry successfully. Tap in and invest in the people. It's not too late to support and change to parallel confinement narrative that urges public to leave mass incarceration in a box like mass graves. What can the White privilege do? Their presence is needed, too. Invest in Incarcerated Lives Matter, tap in to support and employ these Black artists of many hidden talents. It's too much untapped potential, with too much untapped support. Where you all at? We need support for change the wealthy hierarchy of White supremacy. We cannot wait on the one percent to end mass incarceration. We have to break it through these systems of policy break-up reforms.

Systemic is not meaning a mere system. Systemic is of, relating to, or affecting the whole body. Or a systemic pesticide.

Kintsugi is a Japanese word. They use it as their culture. Japanese people fill gold in between things that's broken, like dishes and cups, to see the beauty in broken. Therefore, if their culture and people can find the beauty even in something broken by coincidence or accident, then so can we if we choose to step out of the judgmental society paradigms and adopt Kintsugi practices.

If Nipsey Hussle was alive right now during the social unrest, mass incarceration crisis time, he would have a blueprint and leadership with solutions for the people. The day after Nipsey Hussle was killed, he was supposed to meet with the LA police chief to address Black-on-Black gang violence and talk police reform. They went to Nipsey because they knew he was a leader and came from it. Therefore, who can implement action and root hood problems more than someone with that similar background or experience. I believe Nipsey Hussle would have gave a decathlon ILM creed to model for reform and blueprint. A decathlon is a 10-event athletic contest. That's how you have to work and push inside being incarcerated against all odds and barriers oppression to break through and be heard. If Nipsey showed you all it's a marathon out there, you all had to run and pace yourself for non-stop. Just imagine dealing with corruption, demoralization, and disengagement. This is why, once again, influencers, celebrities, and organizations all need to tap in. Be like Nipsey. Put your money into the hood, ILM, programs, schools, and drug prevention.

By buying and spreading awareness of the message of this book is tapping in showing support and sharing it or sending it to your loved ones incarcerated. Invest in incarcerated lives business loan for the ones that need revenue to kickstart their business plans of food trucks, studios, etc. that a bank wouldn't approve of from lack of credit, work history, and felony. Organizations and companies like Defy Ventures help ex-con men and women get business loans for start-ups. Another organization is HomeBoyIndustries.com and a social enterprise. Health-N-The-Hood organizations that help bring fresh organic food into urban areas as a fresh food market to the Blacks in the community that cannot outsource or commute 45 minutes to suburbs. Even WNBA superstar Mya Moore taking off a whole season including a pay cut to help an incarcerated life injustice that she tapped in to form a Christian church group. Through her passion, assistance, and dedication out of the kindness of her heart for humanity. She did a good deed not for money or to be seen. She tapped in to the pen to support and work her influence and platform to share a spotlight to shine on mass incarceration. She freed a man of over 2 decades of incarceration. He is of the one percent that gets free from all the mass incarceration injustices and systemic racism. Also with cash bail reform all the celebrities like Common, John Legend, Cardi B, and so much more helping all the protestors bail out during the protest of Black Lives Matter that got arrested. Also, all the countless other groups, celebrities, organizations that do things behind the scenes or with their team not to be seen. We all appreciate every ounce of energy, time, capital or efforts. Also teaching ILM how to do code.

By tapping in and having a direct source from within is how we unite and win. Also progress and structure implement on dialogue/reform for outside tools and resources.

Finally, I will emphasize again, invest in Blacks with talent incarcerated to give them jobs and a chance. They need work and housing. Also careers, mentorship, internships contingent upon reentry into society. Gives them fresh out a fresh start and hope. Optimizing for their future and life. It drives their self-reform and recovery process. Building and being there to help catch them, keep free, redirect their focal points, and transition. Just like Nipsey was doing. He got it and hired them, reintegrating them successfully.

If you want to tap in to me personally or help with any endeavors, movements, or funding, my email and contact info is on my About the Author page at the end of this book. If you want to hire me for any speaking events, youth advocates, personal consultants, life coaching, sport events, writing programs, screenplays, personal development seminars, tattoos, etc., I'll be free to come into institutions to help reform, spread the ILM Blueprint and movement. I'll be an ILM advocate and finish building an ILM library.

- Chapter 8 -

"Community Policing & Governing"

Everyone has developed a save-yourself self-mentality. It should not be save yourself, it should be save ourselves, meaning our brothers, sisters, and tribe along with our own community, too. Let's get back to community policing and governing ourselves. Let's fight to hold self-rights and self-accountability. We can push to push the police that's targeting Black communities with racial profiling, arrest boosting, mass incarceration, and killing Black men, women, and children. We can push them out our domestic communities and really police ourselves.

This is the same way that the Native Americans do on their reservations policing and governing with their own tribal police, tribe jails, and laws of the land. No injustices. We need to put people in place that understand our language, us, and our culture. We need people in our community in power or authority like us to help us. First they have to understand us. With race matters it's mixed signals, fear, and misunderstanding. They just paint us Black as evil, trouble, and guilty. We need more grassroot work in the community and powerful and impactful people to step in to help petitions to govern community. We preach and march telling people to vote, but then we walk away from community building. The key is to build a better community for generation to generation for kids, safety, and stop mass killing and incarceration. We have a choice to police ourselves versus accepting the police. Most people do not know a community or county can boycott the police and refuse their services. We can protect ourselves. I challenge you all to look into community policing and policies in your state, county, and district. You can cut police contracts to the community that the city, state, and government funds. Also taxpayers fund, too. The police is contracted out to the communities by the state. The police is nothing but an agency of an entity. Most people don't know this contract exists or that they have a choice and can come together as people of the community to opt out the contract with their local police departments or agencies, including the sheriff department.

We all suffer from not just mass incarceration, we all suffer from mass racism in the community. Plus we all really not free. We have invisible targets on our backs. With recent Kenosha, Wisconsin, police shooting Jacob Blake several times in the back in front of his kids in the car show this is evident. The point is White people have a choice in the morning or in life. Colored people do not. Our Black and Brown brothers and sisters cannot erase this racial invisible target off their backs. However, silently being targeted and haunted in their own backyards, front porches, and community. Therefore, how to stop an invisible enemy and target that you cannot remove off your back is to remove or block that invisible enemy of racism and back targets from the community. Meaning we need to stop them from patrolling the community. No matter how problematic it is or the war on drugs or drug-infested areas, we need fast change relief on police reform. The awareness, education, and visibility needs to be facilitated with strategic ploys and intervention implementation. Again, we can do all this, including digging up these old laws, policies, and statutes to change and establish community independence by unity.

The leaders of the community, dads, and frontline pushers have been victims of systemic racism and incarcerated. They did not abandon or give up on their community. Doc Rivers says it's hard why we love this country, and this country don't love us back. That's true. I say why we love our own people and don't love our community. We need to invest in our community, build our community, and protect our community.

It's over a million frontline pushers and leaders, O.G.s, and fathers locked away from their community. These were our natural chiefs and community protectors dating back to our African tribal communities. Think about if Trump turned on the people like he did with the protestors with military. Or even tweaked the Constitution to enslave all Colored people in a new world executive order. All the warriors, frontline pushers, leaders are locked up. Therefore, you guys are over a million short with aid and protection. Trump does not have a million-man army like China. However, he has over a million Black people incarcerated without no pardons and over 1,100 Black people that get killed in the community by the same officers hand-sworn to protect. Let's wake up on all these issues and push effectively together to police our own community and exile the police department. It's all highly possible if we know how the whole body works thru laws, contracts, and funding. Including these police unions.

Defunding is key, but only one of the key elements. The main goal is to dethrone and departure these police departments and agencies from our community. Google all ways how to sever community from police departments. I'm pretty sure you will see all kinds of data and content. We need to use that same data and content to dismantle them from the roots of community. I know proper preparation prevents poor performances. Therefore, we can save Black lives that all matter—men, women, and children—from being killed or incarcerated, from police misconduct and prosecutorial misconduct. The proof is in the pudding of police community versus us proactively community policing. I rather take action and a chance with us community policing and governing in our own hands than theirs. Our statistics will be an exponential curve compared to theirs of mass graves and mass cages.

You cannot talk lion to a squirrel or weasel to a hyena. They do not frequent to the same surroundings. This is the same for White cops in the community for years, decades, and centuries of racism and unjust acts of violence. It's like oil and water, it does not mix or settle. We cannot just simply end or erase racism from their mental. Babies are not born color-blind and see race. They are open to the world until someone shuts and closes their mind to racism, prejudice, and inequality discriminations.

Let me allow myself to break down governing community. To govern is to regulate, direct, influence, or control your own community. Or you can use it in a technical defined sense, to control and direct the making and administration of policy in rule. We can self-govern and regulate. There is no waiting around for change and for another Black killing or incarceration to weave out the bad seeds by their exclusive actions. We need to uproot the whole plant or plants by self-policing with our own community patrolling, police, and accountability systems into place. We can, too, become a private organization resembling our own police force. Let's completely change directions on our own. Putting time, energy, and unity into play, we can outsource and find our own community enforcers. We, too, can be held to the Constitution and governing laws of society non-biased.

Whereas, community policing is also to control, regulate, or keep in order. Now, the police that's now triggers to everyone's newsfeed due to their misconduct and the systemic racism that plagues our communities like a rotten dead tooth of pain and headache. Police is not engaging and building a connection. They shooting, killing, and incarcerating communities. With our own community policing, we can build connections, love, trust by engaging correctly in the community with respect that's relevant.

Their purpose of police in our community was for the department of government that keeps public order, safety, and enforces the law. Also remember the origin of the police was to capture slaves and police the freed slaves, better known as slave patrol. You have to read your historical black-and-white facts of American Negro history, which we still have yet to overcome and break free from bondage or racism in 2020.

Now, community policing is not nothing new to the table. The original Black Panther Party was doing community policing, building, and feeding. They were organized with structure and woke. Passing community word and spreading community love. People all have their opinions on the Black Panther Party being radical Blacks with rifles. However, they were feeding the community, building community, and community leaders. The Feds had resistance and could not understand the Black evolution of structure, organization, and unity of the Negro. They feared the unity and power of the Black Panther Party that they intervened to break the party up. They tapped their phones, turned parties against each other from other cities. They would lie and brainwash people in their ranks. The operation was illegal and called COINTELPRO. Read about it and educate yourself. My question to you is, where do you think our communities would be if they never broke up the Black Panther community organization? I think in a way better state, with brotherly love and adopted generation practices, brotherhood, sisterhoods, unity, and community value. It's always been about community, giving back, leading, and each one teach one with brotherly love.

The fear the Republican Convention is putting on Black communities is real and perpetuates injustice and racism, not ending racism, violence, prison and police reform. We all need to register to vote. We cannot sit back and watch genocide of Blacks by the hands of police that stalks their community like prey. Trump calls it restoring law and order.

Since 1619 we been going through culture racism and oppression. It's not diverse democracy. Democracy is not doing its work. 47 percent of people that got killed by cops this year (2020) by August were Black men, women, and children. We need essential reform and police removal from community structure plans to succeed.

The question, what tangible can White privilege do? Making a stand and statement with us and using your platforms, influence, or help. Not just wearing a shirt or using a hashtag. We need you all to be proactive, too, and help us address legislators that they must address police reform and press for community change. Stand in solidarity of Black brothers and sisters, too. Not just locking arms and kneeling. Help keep the focus on the issue of racism, reform, and equality. Help your voice be heard on ending mass incarceration. Raise your voice with awareness of getting people registered to vote Trump out of office that promotes violence, racism, and influence the people and systemic racism cops.

Our moral authority, psychology, free assembly, private property, and community are being violated, broken, and traumatized, now and from generations prior in this nation. Our life and lives are something bigger than just us personally. People are not meant to be controlled, caged, killed, suppressed, in a zoo, mentally locked and oppressed. We are meant to be free and have liberty. Not a life of enslavement or treated like wild animals that need to be shot down and killed in the streets. We people of God and meant to break through and live on this planet, breathing air with the same human experience. The human race.

Now, attention all hoods and influencers. Tap in to your O.G.s community and hood leaders. Get the science and math on policing own hoods and community for safety and enforcement with implementation instructions. The urban communities have influence and order from their O.G.s that did hard time, renowned, respected with valid street cred and control. Most of people tweet and get mad, but they do not go out into urban communities in the trenches and streets to stand with the people or assist and guide them. O.G.s, spokesmen, and community representatives all provide direction to the streets and people. Even our community religious leaders and organizations, including community watch party for police prevention, or community organizers, event planners of protest, all have influence in the community and get directly to the people way more effective and powerful than any tweet. We all tribal people and warriors of our community. Yes, the hoods are dysfunctional and the shooting beefs are internal and germinate from within of a concoction of money, drugs, and perpetual retaliation from rival foes they were taught to oppose. You have to live it to understand the hood chain of supply and demand struggle of feeding households poor to save themselves. I understand people of the public see the hood and urban community problematic elements, but have not actually been misfortunate to experience the struggle and condition or toxic environment that you are born in. No excuses or justifying. I am just providing you with a more vivid insight thru my lens personal depth.

Now, the metaphor the blind leading the blind is what happens in our broken family and dysfunctional communities infested with drugs. The kids are left fatherless or abandoned and wards of state and in group homes with mothers absence through drug abuse and neglect. Whereas, due to systemic racism from the cops and criminal justice system, our community leaders are locked down for excessive sentences. Their actions do not deserve 20 years for drug or gun possessions. The O.G.s, leaders, fathers, and brothers of the community being incarcerated lives cause chaos in their absence in the community and indirectly perpetuate Black-on-Black crimes and drugs. Party of supremacy is pinning us against each other, divide and conquer, separating us so that we cannot come together.

To control a community, you need to control their emotions, which is ultimate high with social injustice and COVID pandemic. The demand of the world has pressed us into the realm of distractions of pulls and multitasking or disengagement, which all take your attention, which take your energy. The more scattered your energy, the less you achieve and focus on. Your body follows your mind. How can you get your peak flow daily potential if your mental health depleted? We are innately wired to care for one another in our communities. Love thy neighbor and brothers and sisters of community keepers. Find a man that's diligent in his work and he shall stand amongst kings. One man can lead a nation and feed a village or move the world. Everyone has contributions in one way or another. You never know how significant your contribution can impact community, family, or reform until you push forth effort of value.

How to community build? You start off with support youth, invest youth, feed, clothe, support homeless. Also organic food chains, community watch programs, organizations, enforcers, and youth activities like sporting complexes after school versus hanging out bored in the community. Taking a chance with your people in building your community is better than taking a chance with strangers. All citizens need to educate themselves and use them phones for data research and Google how to do the thing you asking questions to. It's all right there at your fingertips in front of you, too. I understand everyone is at a heightened emotional state, but we must remain united, push, and active, not fatigued and frustrated.

Master P raised $100 million to rebuild his projects, hood, and community that was devastated by Hurricane Katrina. Let's put a public community building fund together like Master P did, too. Celebrities, organizations, influencers come together to build our own communities to remove those police patrol communities that kill or incarcerate Blacks at an all-time high alarming rate. Relocate outside city limits that's not contracted by police department. Our own water source, farming, policing, housing, electric, etc. Look at how the Native Americans do their community policing and use to structure ours as a blueprint despite their reservation being its own entity and laws govern. We can learn a lot by reaching out to the Natives, too, on community building and practices. Natives matter, too.

Lastly, on community policing and building, I wanted to make clear on the Black Panther Party fundamentals and intent. First, the Black Panther Party provided free breakfast and lunch to the kids and people of the community. They also provided free school programs. A fun fact, gangs and the Black Panthers came into existence to protect the community from the police before the Feds dismantled them state to state. This is a past example of community policing and building. We can look at their old blueprint and create our own new modified blueprint. I showed you all different options and routes in this chapter's subject line. However, you can go to the experts and specialists in community build, policing, or planning. I know all activists do not have a plan, but they have a cause and catalyst to push forward. It's up to people to step forward that has that experience to help formulate. Do right by your community to serve. Or we can find people in real time. We have people of color with platforms, influence to get the direct contact to the people we need to reach. To have a victory lap like Nipsey.

NBA Hall of Famer Isaiah Thomas said something interesting. He said, can we just say American versus Black or White, because when you go overseas, they say American. This is to start helping the narrative and seeing visible images of colors and contrasts.

Now that we know all the problems and identify all the pain points, let's apply all the solutions together. Implement plans of actions. We do not have to continue getting bullied by these police in our community. Let's take back our community unified coast-to-coast with restoring, rebuilding, prevention, and action. You know the systemic racism hate what we love. Like Black folks we love to come together, get together, and congregate or eating and function. Just like church, it's love and a harmony of vibration and energy of aura from our innate true spirits.

This same systemic racism is embedded in government, legislature, economics, education, housing, community, and banking loans. We do not have the same equality flat out. Black face, Black status versus White face and White status is privileged with unspoken access. It's hard to win, get ahead when you underpaid, undervalued, discriminated, and hated.

- Chapter 9 -

"Solutions"

"How can you know his heart...when you already judged his skin"
—BeBe Winans, Gospel Artist

"They say the blind will never see...I say yes we can. They say Moses will never part the Red Sea...I say yes we can. They say that the slaves of mass incarceration will never be free...I say yes we can..."—Wyclef Jean

We are too busy on our phones and social platforms for validations. Chasing clout, likes, and popularity for millions following to trend. Neglecting self-building, time, or reflection due to systemic racism making you feel like you don't matter or not loved. You matter, you count, you, too, are deeply loved. Incarcerated lives of government institutions in bondage matter. The best solution on Earth is to know and love thyself. Then you can evolve yourself from personal growth, unity, leadership, and influence as a man or a woman of the community to contribute.

They feel a rise in power of Black excellence and fear being inferior of Black dominance and take over their powerful and political positions. They fear of becoming the minority and we the majority in this country. It's not over order they fear and say they cannot lose, it's really over dominance and control. Remember our country's original sin of enslavement that still has not been redressed. Or the broken promise of Abraham Lincoln's promise of full citizenship, 40 acres and a mule in exchange for fighting for the Union.

Now before I give effective solutions, solution framework, and recommended constructive solutions in this chapter, I would like to address and express this with you all. I won't rest until incarcerated slaves free and these reform bills pass or the Constitution amendment is reframed in its language. I want us to be able to put together a legal task force team in each state and federal to help sort thru these biased injustice cases to overturn these people of mass incarceration from errors and systemic racism victims of the criminal justice system corrupt cash cow entity. I am very dedicated, disciplined, even if it takes the rest of my life to push, organize, and blueprints to be heard and implemented, I will follow thru. Even when I am free.

Also I know this instant gratification era with fast food, fast apps, and fast results, people want immediate actions with immediate results. However, how they have these systems in place, it cannot happen overnight. Part of us formulating successful solutions and plans of action, we must dismantle and attack these White laws they have glued in place to cement themselves with alibis and justification. This is why we have to hire and find people with knowledge and experience in that field to help push and do the work or action that's needed in the solutions. Remember, a slow process is still a progress. Just because you cannot see what's going on behind the scenes does not mean change is not being implemented. You just remember your position and play your part in the push and movement. Excluding cops killing Black lives. They need to immediately be held accountable. There are no shortcuts. We have to perpetually work and challenge ourselves 52 weeks per year to push plans of action for change and reform of police, policy, and prison.

Let's get into it. Remember, this whole book, we have identified all the problems and troubleshoots. We also have laid out solution framework at the end of the chapters, too. Incarcerated Lives Matter, Black Lives Matter united to push both sides of the flipped coin from the police in the communities of systemic racism. Social and criminal justice reform known as police and prison reform. An ILM Blueprint for the incarcerated men, women, and juveniles to find self, reform, and transition. Community policing, governing, and building. Influencers tapping into mass incarceration and the community. Voting during COVID pandemic and voter suppression. First solution is forget about following pop culture and learn, invest into Black culture to help create change. You cannot play your part united with us if you do not know what's going on with us. To all, including White privilege that stand with our reform movements. Remember, it's two crises in 2020 we fighting against—racism and COVID pandemic—that disproportionately kill more Blacks in both ways. It's also an election year, our greatest challenge for a shift and immediate change of reform.

It's time for a new convo and new solutions. Our solutions are not their solutions. An example of this is Breonna Taylor and Jacob Blake Jr. Our solution is to arrest the officers responsible. Their solution is to investigate or fire. I find it ironic and a slap in the face how Jacob Blake Jr. lies paralyzed, handcuffed to a hospital bed after being shot several times. It's obvious he cannot go or run nowhere. They say it's standard procedure. Their standard procedure is not ours. Our standard procedure is to handcuff the officer, not the Black man victim. This what the outcry is all about. The two justice systems, the White one and the Black biased one of all injustices. We need to dismantle police playbook of how to get away with murder of Negroes. Saying they fear for their lives, make objects weapons or plant them, assassinate them and their character. Then turn on the protestors by attacking them for putting the police on blast. This is why Jacob Blake Senior says we, the Colored people, hold our own court and find them cops all guilty for all misconduct even if they get acquittal or not charged. It's true and just our realization that we want to project for the whole world to see the greatest nation what they call humanity.

After Trayvon Martin shooter Zimmerman got acquitted on murder charges of a Black child, 3 Black girls created the slogan Black Lives Matter! That same year I was so moved and touched, I had to use my superpower to write a book called *If Trayvon Martin Could Talk; Injustice*, which I never got it published into print for his parents' approval because I was short funded and sent it to someone to type and help that fell flat. I still kept writing as an inside advocate and activist thru my books and push.

Let's do an all-Blackout total push and boycott. Not just a Tuesday online Blackout. All of us boycott together on one specific day for however long it takes to get the message, attention, and plan of action implemented into real time valid solutions. Everybody must be involved and participate for success rates. All essential workers, developers, sanitation, healthcare, food processing, jobs, athletes, influencers, etc. What most people do not realize how much power we really have because we are too codependent on them or others. We built this country with blood, sweat, and tears. They took over and stole this country. It's okay to think outside the box. Jeff Bezos just hit $200 billion with Amazon. We, too, can build our own platforms by thinking outside the box. Think about it and look at it this way: We are the heart of the economy. The spenders, the buyers, the investors, the advertisers, the trendsetters, the fashion statements. However, we are not the shareholders, business owners of the higher billion-dollar entities. We fuel their stocks buying all their fast food, junk food, brands, etc. What if we start our own food chains, organic channels, and our own leagues, like Ice Cube Big 3, FUBU—for us, by us, meaning all Black-owned banks, businesses, brands, products, and services exclusively? We shut down their markets and platforms and create our own sole proprietor or proprietress. If we clog their economy, they will be running to us with effective reversal and universal solutions. Plural solutions and reform advocates and policies jumping out the trees, when we defund, dismantle, or stop their cash flow and hit their wallets. Just like we can build and police our own community, we can build our own marketplaces, economy, and healthcare practices. This is all thinking solutions. If you can imagine it, you can formulate it. If you can see it, someone else can believe it and achieve your vision or share your vision to someone else that is an expert in what you visualize, concoct, or integrating. All is possible. Again, we need to gather people who have experience in the solutions plan of action. We need to have dysfunction and eruption to spark change in the systems they have bestowed in place for us not to bypass.

We cannot take the focal points off the issues. We had limited opportunities since day one we still trying to climb out of. Protest peaceful is progress, demonstrating and to be heard. A plan has to be in place like the NBA boycott, NFL, WNBA, MLB, and Osaka, the tennis player, did. Influencers that can promote and provoke change. They got millions of eyes and ears tapped in to influence and catch the lawmakers', mayors', governors' attention. With organizations and billion-dollar boys' club corporations, having a seat on the board of directors is all possible to break through to. Move from stigmas to constructive solutions. Sociologists say how do we use or message attention to leverage change? Let's talk about equality solutions: economics, education, housing, healthcare, microfinance, equal pay, and justice. Lobbyists get paid for influencing people in power to push bills. Who can be lobbied or leveraged? Shooting and killing unarmed Black men, women, and children should be passed as a federal hate crime to these police and all vigilantes or extremist groups, citizens like Ahmaud Arbery or Trayvon Martin cases. Reform police unions, its systemic injustice. The secret police force, too, that really exists. The same ones responsible that were unidentified, pushing protestors out of the way and spraying them with tear gas for Trump photo op with Bible in front of a burnt-up church. We need to end police qualified immunity.

They remove sorting machines from certain urban areas so we cannot mail-in votes. The entrenched party don't want you to vote. You must vote. Vote on municipal, state, and federal levels. Commit to voting for change. Commit to serving the community. Standing at them polls, masked up in the cold even when your legs are tired. Stand tall for us all. Reverend Al Sharpton NationalActionNetwork.com, you can go to sign up to be a poll watcher to protect the ballot votes in your city or state. Therefore, please tap in to the community networks and to register to vote. These are all part of the solutions to implement, which helps in the process of eliminating systemic racism. The John Lewis bill act pass voting rights bill by Congress to pass, which they gutted out the right to vote in 2013 that we fought for. Therefore, we must push our votes to get it reinstated until it's federal regulation in every state. All the dignity we've been denied. Also, the Breonna Taylor bill pass of no-knock search warrants federal throughout nation. The George Floyd bill act pass banning chokeholds and deescalating tactics federal, too. The HBYO reparations passed, too. Then we must demilitarize the police and add racial bias training. Dismantle criminal justice system with the power of Black coalitions and politics. Keep social justice movement going, criminal justice movement going, Black unity, Black freedom, and Black equality. When you pivot from this to that is how you transition for effective solutions. Reparations means to amend a wrong with compensation for damages caused.

Programs online, newsfeed, and TV talk you into wars, lies, and propaganda for ratings, not truths. Even spiritual and false prophets, long as we do not emotionally react. The known is the norm order. Chaos is out of order. Therefore, peace projects in community, the violence goes down. Creates unity. We have to use whatever megaphone, voice, platform, writing, books, art, social sharing to be heard. Especially that you do not get to talk about that message needs not to be silent, it needs to be pluralized. Intervention, psychotherapy needs mental health experts.

Prison companies that are profiting off collect calls or adding money to the pre-paid accounts off of mass incarcerated Black families. Including private prison commissary companies need to be defunded and stripped down contracts from the prison, too, as a solution. By defunding private prison commodities, phone vendors, and commissary vendor chains, we break or suspend their contracts to the private prisons and state prisons, we dismantle their profit margins, cut their exploitation, and expose their budget cut personal profiting and gains in their pockets. It's a big business the prison allows these outsourced private vendors to tax, price gouging, and getting profits off commissary and vendors sales contract, which they shake down Black families of mass incarceration to feed, and keep an open line of communication with their loved ones. If you want to get to the heart of something, you have to get inside just like a doctor or journalist. Mass incarceration is an

American crisis that locks up more people than any other country. It's not working and a broken system. People praise the punishment model. America needs to stop thinking punishment, especially to innocent, racial bias profiled, petty crimes, and over-punishing people that don't deserve it. Start thinking from punishment to rehabilitation. All the false claims of Department of Corrections are not correcting nothing. Evidently, it's false advertisement to the public display. This is why our mission is to end and dismantle with our solutions to prison reform.

And still we stand tall, united we shall rise above all, and never fold or fall. We want to tackle the penal system as a whole. Police feels like street justice and it's their job to punish us, it's the judge's job to hand down sentences. However, they are in cahoots with the courts district and county attorneys. Despair in unfair margins Blacks to Whites incarceration. Mental health, homelessness, which biased judges and attorneys still throw the book at needs to be stopped, and track all bias patterns and abuse of power. Do a data track and trace spreadsheet just like they implement for COVID-19. However, do an overview of all misconduct on judges, lawyers, prosecutors, and cops. Diverse jury pools are a problem that we need to simplify to fix. We can put a simple diversity team at all jury selection processes and during jury instructions to prevent due process violations and prejudiced trial convictions, mass incarceration.

It's time to move the conversation forward and action further for leadership solutions. 10 percent of Blacks in their thirties in jail in the U.S. It's 2 changes, policy changes and culture changes, are the tip of the iceberg. Public education, healthcare, and minority employment are the aim, too. What's the solution to move forward is to tackle the main ones, judiciary, equality, and systemic racism with unity. Then, attack Black-on-Black violence, reverse the old Willie Lynch blueprint for the Negro slaves that caused further post-slavery generational passed down mental effect. They have been using the divide-and-conquer with mass incarceration breaking communities, homes, and families stirring up waters. Then we are still drunken and deluded us to believe we are enemies and not blood brothers. It is really time to unite, us against them. Our self-worth, self-reform ILM and BLM, educate, love self and each other. Do not compromise the main principles. Be steadfast, proactive, and unwavering, and stand firm in solidarity with unity. Pull all Black leaders to move forward as a nation. Let's change environments, liquor stores, smoke shops, etc. in the community. All Trump's lies, hidden tweets, message and promote engagement of systemic racism. They want to block the vote for them to elect the extremist racist people in power to cut healthcare, benefits, and wages, plus rules to keep them rich and in power. It's more prisons than schools and money into prisons versus education and schools.

Racial justice, racial equality is the push solution. We all have a voice to be heard, placed into incarceration have forced-silenced us. Let's open the net as a whole with ILM, too. Legal defense funds and charity funds for ILM. Use this spotlight as a portal to break through. Do petitions to sign for city council to put into play or ballots. Have influencers use their platforms to share movement. Help condemn criminal justice racism. Redemption and criminal justice reform. Police have to change their behavior and tactics. Enslaved bodied Blacks. Prosecutor misconduct racism and public defenders sell you out using a fear tactic with a timetable chart of projected harder jail sentences if you do not plea bargain out, with false negatives to sign your freedom away, violating rights. Bringing up prior convictions to enhance your time. Threaten you to allege those prior convictions if you go to the trial box. Also, those same prior convictions you served debt to society for already. Gives you double time.

You guys been pushing and fighting BLM out there, and we have been pushing and fighting ILM inside of here. Challenging any BLM activist to tap in and reach out or unite with a prison reform organization or Brian Stevenson. Again, challenging all influencers to establish and invest in lockdown society, prison reform, excessive sentencing, and being crushed, lost, or abused in the penal system. Let's change the narrative they locked-up and guilty, oh well! Let's start reaching back out with a hand to help them up and get out. The divided between— nobody gets left behind if we want to rebuild and restore protecting the community like the Panther party sought. Our lockdown society reform tactics, each one teach one, educate, elevate, innovate, accountability, responsibility, work ethics, community relations, brotherly/sisterly love, and unity is all our key solutions inside to do a constructive 180.

New implements, new tactics, and special funds for law students, firms, and lawyers and legal organizations to review and overlook, investigate all bias, excessive cases, especially with police misconduct and prosecutor misconduct that match a pattern behavior of systemic racism against minorities. Especially locking them up.

A healed gang member does not go back to prison. They need help with transformation and transforming. We as O.G.s train, advise, counsel, and guide with order. People that have mental issues, trauma, all can be helped. Tenderness is the highest form of love to help. Also a model that holds people. Changing behavior is hard. Change the environment, enable successful change of behavior and habits. You must get out of those same reoccurring toxic environments for better outcome, or you get the same exact results. Therefore, curate a good environment for the best effective growth solutions. Show me your close friends and I will show you your future. Remember, it's our points of view and their narratives.

Do not allow people's limitations to limit you or kill your dreams because theirs are. To show people and ILM they can and anything is possible. The example of self-reform and help with transition. Like Nipsey Hussle making people see it's all possible and believe in themselves. The movements make change. Puts life into perspective and to start within to fix the problem of ILM and don't abandon them. To help each other correct themselves. Again, just like Maya Moore from WNBA helped get Jonathan Irons out and free by dedicating a whole season off.

This intersection of BLM and ILM from cops' misconduct needs a united thought process to reform. All police and prison reform solutions for starters. Then focal points for equality overall these systemic racism systems. Look after all bias jurisdictions, including judge, lawyer, and prosecutor conduct. All to bust up their systemic racism. Get better prison programs and projects to educate and rehabilitate. Start freedom justice projects for overturning cases. Ex-cons get out unable to get jobs, interviews because of their felony mark or rap sheet. Or rights to vote and bear arms due to cops' racism and targeted profiling. Also homeless reentry. A data history. Get police officers' records of misconduct and behavior patterns, arrest history, and make it retroactive to all. Prosecutor misconduct bias cases and judges' abuse or discretion power. Including all old cases forgotten over the years, people inside suffered from injustices stuck to rot. We are truly forgotten in the penal system, oblivious that we still exist to society. We have to start fresh as a solution. Kick old officials bias and racist in penal justice system out that's cancerous. They feed the machine clogging the criminal justice system with overflow of mass incarceration.

Unrest and looking outside from a barred cage in rage. We all get taken from our children, dead, or in jail. Remember, judges help keep errors down, not to overturn cases because one case can free up a hundred thousand retroactive. The outside is not aware of how the legal system and technicalities hold us incarcerated down. Also remember the Brady's list was designed to track all police citations data and misconduct. We need to have our own independent source of police misconduct and prosecutor, judge misconduct data tracking systems in place as intervention for the best solutions to minimize systemic racism effectively and directly. It's definitely time for a judicial system shift of implementation and accountability to dismantle bias with prison and criminal reform. Yes, once again slavery was the first U.S. sin and we were the essential slaves that built the labor force. The amendment of slavery in Constitution is to be abolished incarceration for government slaves. Once we get them to rewrite the language of Constitution amendment to remove that key underlined "slave" word, they can no longer hold us in mass incarceration captured until they reframe the language. Maybe to rehabilitation or to reform. Either it creates a space or loopholes for our powerful leaders and professionals in the position of power to rewrite it or a supplement and creed. It's the laws that they segue to hold us and market us on a modern-day slave auction block that they hold their hands up and shrug their shoulders to smirking devilishly. We need to really put people in power who are for us versus enforcing same systemic systems. We want retribution and all cold case police homicides of Blacks. We need a special unit division assigned to look over all these cases and encourage all ex-retired police officers to come forward and hold others accountable and any cover-ups. For the families, and do it for humanity. Do not take your guilt and someone else's unjust blood to your grave. Accountability is key and standing up to show your true conscience and character. Most Black families and mothers never even got a sorry and apologies before or after they buried their loved ones or sons and daughters of the communities from police murders.

This is why we must vote. Votes are quid pro quo. All facets of the Black community. Dismantle this whole systemic White supremacy. You all can't breathe out there and we can't speak in here. There are a lot of us with leadership and direction in us. However, that does not make us an infinite leader. Everybody in our urban society and culture has a role and a position to play. From professionals, thinkers, leadership skills, advocates, and activists. We have to elect the right leaders that care passionately for the people to push as best solutions. Transparency, trust in process, and effective tools. From mayors, city council, prosecutors, senators, etc. of Colored people and diversity are all needed. Also your First Amendment right to protest and push new systems implementations.

Finally, the solution is to reform from federal and state level. From mayors to police chiefs. Essential codes. Respect for humanity and a moral compass. You cannot train for that, accountability. Police union chiefs block all access and accountability data, protecting the cops of their union. We need to stop this and defund police union and city contracts. The cops get arrested but not convicted. We get arrested and convicted with all type of due process violations and end up with excessive sentences. That White woman police officer in Texas came home from work, claims she smelled weed, kicked open her Black neighbor's door eating ice cream and shot him with a vital kill shot thru the heart. She got sentenced to 10 years for least murder charge.

I got 12 years for stripping someone down of their belongings and 10 years for a shooting in the feds. Ask yourself, how does that happen? It's a simple answer, a mere color barrier in this corrupt broken system of mass incarceration and systemic racism cash cow of live human storage facilities. Predominantly Blacks. We all matter, Black lives, kids, women, men, and incarcerated lives, too.

Then the key goal is to spread awareness and push the movement to petition the right people in office to drop a bill in Congress to rewrite the U.S. Constitution amendment and abolish government institution slavery. Know and believe this Constitution was written by their slave owner and prejudiced forefathers and not for the Negro. Make them recognize it and fix it. The word "slave" should not be in the Constitutions or their mouths, period. Most of us plagued with this hood and thug environment syndrome of a struggle. Layers of oppression to where you cannot breathe figuratively. Oppression and inequality elephant in room and issue people do not want to talk about or address because of taboo pulling the race card. It is about humanity, race is an issue. Voices simply not heard, valid, or accepted from own community or society and to the world muffled from injustices. We need valid reform solution to be in place and implement to successfully reform.

I will leave you all with a few more solutions. Fix up community homes and offer free housing upon reentry and non-profit to help fund, or GoFundMe pages. It is going to be someone from ILM to break through. I already started, used prison as my platform to push and reform, and the face of the ILM movement. Also effective reentry programs and plans.

Lastly, solutions to help you self-reform, whether incarcerated or free, for betterment. Help self-reform, believe in self, learn self, grow, and develop skillsets. Get computer literacy, code your own software programs, design own apps and virtual games or A.I. (Artificial Intelligence). They are the future. Then, read or listen to Audibles.

5 key principles are commitment, self-discipline, consistency. Faith that if you do right stuff and self-reform, it will pay off, even though you cannot see it, you got mindset. And the last one is heart. You have to find strength to give more when you are tapped out, you keep pushing through. No matter how hard or tough, your breakthrough will happen. Even if it's in community or a farfetched goal, if you have the heart and mindset, you can reach and achieve it regardless.

Practice self-awareness and play into your strengths, put the work in, period. Like Kobe Bryant says, once you put in so much work, people cannot catch up to you because you are too far ahead and put in too much time for them to duplicate your work ethic and push. Practice working on your weakness. Practice observing, learning, and listening. The process of development.

Consciousness, seek knowledge perpetually, and have discipline. Break bad habits and accord good habits. Please self-educate and read to all the Black youth and folks. Even watching educational videos, seminars, and webinars all work and help your journey of transformations. Think creatively, critically, innovatively, and independently. Always be creating and push your superpowers. Process to creativity is clearing your mind.

Always know linear is a flat line and the same without no growth. Exponential steps, growth doubling or faster rate of accelerating return. Shock value is the ability to progress at a faster rate. We need an inflection point solution. Example exponential technology is disruptive taken-down companies and over like Kodak and Instagram, Blockbuster and

Netflix, Uber, and 3D printers, too. The dematerialize and demonetize things is how you knock down big billion-dollar entities. This same disruptive behavior is the push solution to defund, dismantle, and disrupt for prison and police reform.

Ushered in the world of greed, corruption, inequality, a mass incarceration you have inherited. The Constitution illustrates the complexity of this American system. It serves the interests of a wealthy elite. They enable the elite to keep control with a minimum of coercion, a maximum of law.

The first step in beating a system as powerful and organized as judicial system is understand the basis of law and their power. It also comes with a blind side and loopholes. Why is this system implemented if you cannot win or beat them by no means to try to make it fair and unbiased when it is very prejudiced to delinquent people and target certain people, places, and acts? When you analyze opponent beyond the superficial to the point of vulnerability on which their power is based, striking this point will inflict disproportionate damage. It must be understood that radical social change is no different than warfare, and warfare is a form of power.

Power systems share the same basic structures. The most visible thing about them is their appearance, what is seen and felt. The outward display of repressive power is a deceptive fabrication, a manifestation of insecurity, since power dares not expose its weakness. The key lies in determining what their point of vulnerability is and to do so, you must understand the structure of the power system and the culture in which it operates. The importance in American democracy is the social and political support of its citizens. The court system in this country is increasingly becoming an important tool of repression on behalf of the exploiters.

We need full employment with a living wage for all people who will work. The U.S. Declaration of Independence states in part "that all men...are endowed...with certain inalienable rights; that among these are life, liberty and the pursuit of happiness. That to secure these rights, governments are instituted among men, deriving their just power from the consent of the governed." Life is a right and thus the means to live, work, and making a living wage all must be equally guaranteed. If corporate business will not provide full employment even as they sit on trillions of dollars fleeced from the surplus value of labor, then the means of production should be taken from them and placed into the community.

We need affordable, equal access to higher education for all. We need education that teaches the true history of colonialism, chattel slavery, repression of organized labor, police repression, and imprisonment as tools of capitalist exploitation and the perpetuation of imperialism in the U.S. power system and corporate financial markets. Speculative profiteering drives up tuition, leaving most in debt and pricing higher education out of reach for communities of the poor. Usurious student debt should be forgiven in full.

We need an end to all corporate and financial influences in the political process in the U.S. The nature of U.S. society has been of the rich, for the rich, and by the rich. This marginalizes the people. The U.S. will finally become a nation of the people, for the people, and by the people, where only individual citizens have influence in the democratic process. Ban all lobbyists, donors, and special interest groups from local, state, and federal electoral and legislative process.

We need an end to imperialist wars of aggression and sending our youth off to kill and die to enforce the economic interests of big oil and other corporate concerns and as an impetus to keep from addressing domestic ills.

We need an end to the prison industrial complex as a profit base, from our tax dollars, for the disposal of surplus labor and the poor. We need an end to solitary confinement, torture units, and the U.S. mass incarceration of people of color and the poor will no longer be tolerated. The prison population in the U.S. has exploded 600 percent since 1981. The continued indefinite confinement of human beings stored in AZ SMUs like my current situations, CA SHUS, and other supermax torture units in the Feds must be immediately abolished. True rehabilitation, such as vocational programs, access to higher education, and community-based parole boards must become the new order of the day. Also computers, putting computers in all the prisons so those inside can learn and build careers with computer networking and entrepreneurship for their own business online and from home without worrying about other companies' job discrimination or working in a biased workplace.

We need an end to all institutional racism, race- and class-based disparities in access to and quality of labor education, healthcare, criminal defense, political empowerment, technology, and healthy food. Structural features of capitalism prevent broad cooperation between 99 percent from various racial, ethnic, and cultural backgrounds. We will no longer allow this divide-and-rule arrangement to govern our relationships.

We need decent and affordable housing for all people. Housing is a fundamental necessity. However, the government has consistently sided with Wall Street and the Fed, who are responsible for the greatest loss of housing in the nation's history. Federal, state, and local officials criminalize homelessness and poverty. The government should mandate a readjustment of home equity debt on all U.S. homes so what people owe reflects what the properties are now worth. Empty Federal Housing Authority properties should be made into co-ops so communities can create decent housing for all.

We need an immediate end to police brutality and the murder of oppressed people in the U.S., particularly in the Black, Latino, immigrant, and underclass communities. Also among those protesting in this nation. We recognize the police and other state paramilitary agencies are and always have been the enforcement army of the ruling 1 percent. We recognize such brutal and unwarranted lethal treatment is the daily existence of Blacks, Latinos, immigrants, and underclass urban communities and people in this nation. Self-defense is a human right. Community-organized oversight and self-defense forces should be organized to monitor and record police and defend the people with mando body cams. We will suffer no more attacks like those of Ahmaud Arbery at UC Davis, no more George Floyds, Scott Olsens, and Oscar Grants, nor to be injured like Rodney King and shot up like Jacob Blake Jr., or Trayvon Martin, Breonna Taylor, Kendrec McDade, and Jason Smith, killed by the tools of the 1 percent.

We really need a bottom-up approach to economic development and labor-capital relations in the U.S. The state has aligned itself so intimately for so long with the interest of the ruling 1 percent that it has become enamored exclusively to a top-down approach. This has resulted in a 281 percent growth of wealth in the top 1 percent of this nation. While the bottom 99 percent have seen their income flat over 20 years. We must now uplift the quality of life from the bottom rung up, empowering the disenfranchised, and directing bailouts and subsidies to the people, not banks and billionaires.

We need a more equitable distribution of wealth, justice, and opportunity at every level of society, too. There is enough food that no one needs to be hungry. There are enough unoccupied structures that no one needs to be homeless. We have enough educators, institutions, knowledge, and technology that no one needs to be without a degree or skilled trade. There is enough work to be done that no one needs to be without a job. Only the stranglehold of the super-rich 1 percent on every institution and apparatus of this nation's infrastructure ensures that their opulence and White privilege of generational wealth are maintained at the expense of the 99 percent.

There are some 47 million people in America living below the poverty line. Another 150 million or so barely getting by. Especially now after the COVID pandemic those numbers tripled. Which is almost two-thirds of the nation's population. All part of the 99 percent. It is here that we will find our most lasting support. Thus are overwhelmingly Blacks, Latinos, immigrants, and poor communities.

These solutions are a protracted struggle; victory will require sacrifice, tenacity, and competent strategic insight.

Therefore, your greatest power lies in your unity, cooperation, and ultimately your organizational ability. The power of the people far surpasses all the repressive violence attacking you/us, surpasses the wealth of the 1 percent, who will stop at nothing to silence us all.

Therefore, I encourage all minorities, Black, Latino, immigrants to vote on November 3rd, 2020, elections, state and federal local levels, too. However, make sure you vote once, either the polls or mail-in votes. You cannot vote twice like Trump telling people to do. However, the biggest solution plan of action to be effective is to get the White privilege and other independent parties to vote in our favor and swing their votes with us. This is the dialogue, and a shift of environments, unrest, and racial disparity that split this country. Show them why it will be beneficial to swing on the Biden and K. Harris campaign for betterment of both interests, ours and theirs, too. Again, we cannot win with just the 17 and 14 percent of the minorities, Black and Latino voters, we need others. Start networking and reaching out to who you can share viewpoints, common knowledge, and race relationship. Also inequalities.

- Chapter 10 -

"Universal Connection & Awareness"

"A mastermind...First you master the grind...Then your team catch it." —Nipsey Hussle the Great

This is the last chapter of the book. Thank you for tapping in and listening to my journey, movement, blueprint, and voice for all ILM to push and end mass incarceration. I was able to freestyle this book in 3½ weeks total. No extensive research or online research, just me picking my own brain and retrieving knowledge, freestyling one of my many superpowers. All of this is possible thru my universal connection. This is how I broke down about in the ILM Blueprint chapter about tapping into self and elevating your consciousness. I will give you some universal connection tools to help enable you on your journey and innate path of connection to the world of vibration and energy. Also to find your strengths thru self-awareness, aka awaken.

However, before you get started in this framework and tools, I would like to share with you a fun fact to add some humor to make you smile and show gratitude for your outside life and freedom of choices versus us restricted movement and no choices or say in power on the inside. Okay, right now I am eating a dry-ass bologna sandwich, for which in jail we call a bologna sandwich a poor man's steak, LOL! I grew up in the projects, so I'm humbled to share with you all I'm not too prideful. This is my reality and self-actualization. When you hungry, the stalest or greenish bologna can taste like the tenderest Omaha steak. My heart still beating and I'm still breathing, plus I woke up this morning is all the gratitude I need. On top of me being in an institution, but not institutionalized. I'm locked up and down like death row inmates 25/8, no sunlight in over 2 years. However, I can smile and sleep like a king even with my illegal sentence error I suffer from because my mind is totally free! Truly, this is how I am able to write and hit key notes that you feel and cannot articulate or manifest from within. It's called universal connection and awareness. Let's get into it.

Remember, gratitude first. Be thankful for life, breath, and that God-given universal light, spirit, or consciousness you have within you that's aligned just like the stars and Milky Way in our galaxy. Except you need to push and tune your aura energy to the universal frequency. Yes, I said the universe has a clear frequency that everything inside it vibe to. Just like the internet connects us all right there in our pocket or at our fingertips. However, we still innately disconnected. Let's connect our movements, connect our actions, and connect our solutions universal with awareness. How about that? It's all possible with unity. In the '60s their generation pushed with unity. The marches, stands, protests, etc. Even the ones that got killed or our ancestors, we still have a united generation that did a universal push to keep their leadership, message, dream, and blueprints alive on this Earth. We must evolve this movement into the universal push united to get universal results.

What separates us as humans from animals is intellect. Animals have instinct. Even when they use their brains to maneuver a new way or to evolve, it's still instinct that adopts that newly discovered primal instinct. We need to get out of the automated impulsive and instinct mode. Then tap into the realm of intellect to connect. Remember, you are the original man and woman of color and people, period. That means you were the creators and creatives of the origin of this world. Them pyramids are part of Africa and your ancestors that were universal connected that had pyramids all over the world, just Google pyramids to see. Before we were enslaved, stripped of knowledge, religion, culture, tribal traditions, self-worth, we were connected universal to the world. Now we disconnected universal, and they have enslaved our minds. If you claim you woke, you cannot be if you haven't woke nobody else or cannot wake universal. A universal connection and awareness will awake the whole world and vibrate the universe. We, the original men and women, are so affluential and vibrant, it's contagious and gets the whole world to move. Black is not dark, Black is universal power. Our whole world, universe, galaxy system was built out of Blackness. Blackness from nothing to universal light. That same light, earthly elements inside of us all, the same elements of stardust, oxygen, nickel, iron, carbon, and even H_2O. It's in all of us, else you wouldn't be a human or an inhabitant of this Earth. From every atom, organism, insect, to animals. We all one universe and innately connect with the same mechanics, aura energy and heart-beating vibrations.

Have you ever noticed how two Black people can have a White baby, blonde hair, or an albino? However, two White people cannot have an actual Black baby. Black genes are predominantly stronger and dominant. This is why we are more sculpted with muscle definition or curves. Excel in all fields, including sports dominance. They enslaved us for their labor because of our strength and endurance, including the Black woman's exclusive strenuous strength endurance. It's not just childbirth labor, women naturally have more pain endorphins and are subjectable to higher tolerance to pain. Black women can endure struggles. That does not mean they should have to because they can absorb it. We need our queens to exist and push their universal energy, too. We all have sexual energy, spiritual energy, connectedness, super conscious energy, and natural daily energy. It's up to what you put this energy into. Whether negative energy draining you and subtracting from the universe, or positive energy that's building and adding to the universal law of vibrations and frequency. I showed you in the blueprint how to tap into this and be creative. We all our creators and have creative energy sources. We apply our energy to others and give up our thriving energy to others' toxicity and strenuous negative activity. This is what you need to be able to Toosie Slide to like Drake do after you feel their negative vibrant beat. Rhythm and flow is real and universal. This is who we are, able to dance together to one hit song thru vibrations.

Now, do not get lost in the Sriracha sauce. I am just being transparent what universal connection is. Now we need to use it together and get on the same frequency to reverse the polarity from negative to positive. Therefore, for us, the universal connection is to restore power into the people by letting them know first, they have and possess the power within to shift and move the universe. Then push together as a movement on the same frequency to relinquish people with power over you. Most people do not take the time out to recognize the actualization that people only have power over them because they allow them to by giving and relinquishing their power to them. Again, do not give things, people your power or entertain it. We are so disconnected with all these social platforms designed to keep you engaged in their space instead of your own place. They are the best tech specialists and design algorithms to feed and play into your psyche and short attention span. They say a goldfish's attention span is the equivalent of 6 seconds. Now studies show human's attention span is less than a goldfish, 4-5 seconds. Think about it. When was the last time you sat and thought about connecting or pondering on something righteous anyway? Most people only think after the fact of why they did not connect with that other person after the relationship over or why they not making connections at their dates. It's because you have to have the right mindset to tune into the right frequency.

How can you vibe or be on someone else's frequency if you cannot connect to yours? You have to find self or self frequency first. Before you can make a universal connection, you have to be connected to the universe with self. If we pushing a movement together, it does not matter if he is from the UK or France as long as he feels me, my energy and vibrations, he's nodding his head and protesting or pushing too because our universal connection, it automatically creates energy for universal awareness, too. Google trains a team of entrepreneurs to think every day on how to solve something new or innovate new ideas that most are not trained to think about or outside of the box. They have a framework for their think tanks and innovation by writing down as many ideas, visions, solutions, that's all simplified as possible. These innovators are aware and tapped into their universal connection. You can do this, too. Write down all you want to say, do, fix, or simplify, and then push it into universe for it to come into existence, like the Bible says. Remember the level 4 stage of conscious connectedness to tap into, known as the God mind, which, again, is total connectedness to everything, no limits, and elevation for bending reality or laws of universe with connectedness and intuition. You have to truly elevate consciousness to tap in. Also have a true sense of universal connectedness to tap into true intuition.

Let's finish building on this and awareness. Mentorship and apprenticeship are how people passed down information and traditions from generations. Therefore, you can, too, with universal awareness and connectedness. Multiplication is better than adding. Do a process to set up your 50 to 80 years of work to multiply, connect, or awareness for 200 to 300 years in the universe from now. Bestow your system, message, and connectivities to perpetuate into the universe. Two thousand years later Jesus is still perpetuated into the universe. Build processes that last and infinite multiplier. Just the same as building generational wealth.

Show all is possible. Invest in connectedness universal ideas and visions to help change people. Create a base, follow it, and grow, accomplish, reward, and rejoice it. My goal is to plant a universal seed of reform, self-awareness into the universe and universal to all, which is the seat of this book seed I sow. If you are an expert, you have skill, knowledge. How to extract your knowledge just like I do out of prison. Then you build a community, share it, make impact, and connect it to the universe for it to multiply and perpetuate, it will catch on. Curate your energy, vision, or information you want to push forth universal. People love to collaborate energy and be a part of a universal community. Make universal connections the new norm. Self-educate, meditate, and delegate.

Remember, you have to access the fulfilment of results you wish outcome in the universe first. Then the attachment will go away. Then you just focus on creative niche and pumping out positive energy vibrations and masterpieces, priceless.

"Life is more precious than platinum or gold. Don't gain the world and lose your soul..." —Bob Marley

Once you abundance to self, people will come, money and the world will bend the universe around you and within you. Facts. If it contracts you or expands you? Your pros and cons, which saying no to a lot of things, including self. We live second highest and miss out on the universe and universal true connection. Infinite powers.

Help you birth a new consciousness, connection, and show you self-discipline. How to put in the hard work and practice, self-awareness. From working out habits, to healthy and conscious eating habits and choices. Connect to you, clear the social media and world clutter and junk of repression to tap into the universe embodied in you and around you. In America you can do what you want and be what you want to be, except in jail, where they prohibit growth. However, you can do this naturally, not just in America of opportunity, but within the universe and self you can be whatever or do whatever you push your energy into the universe in.

Stop justifying your ideas from delusion and fear, like saying your dreams and ideas you push into the universe is impossible because of this or that and dismissing them. Do not move based on fear or others, please don't. Eliminating self-doubt being locked up is control. They say we better not do what they do not want you to do. They try to lock up your soul and mind. The more you try to control anyone or anything, you are the one being controlled.

People follow patterns daily of self-routines and programs mentally that you rehearsed. You can be institutionalized too from the inner institutions of your own ego, pride, and mental focus or universal connection. You can be repressing yourself indirectly. It is the identity you create. People cry from realization from seeing or waking up that the story you're seeing or believing is not true. You pick up traits or create a false identity when you can cry out yourself. Facts do not care about feelings like an unseen inner child. It's not you, it's an old version of you. Do not give people the power of repression over you and feel like you do not matter.

You got to get into yourself, away from your patterns programmed by parents and society. A win is abundance, are they fulfilled, the consciousness of the world and universe. We're so repressed, understand you're the abundance, not money. The achievement overcomes the fear and use it as a driver or catalyst. The highest vibration and universal connection to ourselves is best. Nobody do not look at the source where the money came from us, the money. The old structures are not working. The conscious meditate and listen to self universal connection.

On the news a state highway patrolman saw a driver on the expressway swerving outside lanes. Pulled over a 5-year-old in his parents' minivan. The boy stated he was driving to California to buy a Lambo with 3 dollars in his pocket. The highway patrol and his parents, along with the world, was in shock. A football player was moved by the 5-year-old's story and let him ride in his Lambo with him. Now the purpose of this story is to point out the power of universal connection and awareness. This is what the 5-year-old tapped into rather accidentally, influenced or innately purposed to push out into the universe and connect the Lambo to him. If a 5-year-old can access his universal connection power, then so can you, too, tap in.

That same day on the news, I saw another headline story of a highway patrol pulled to the side of the highway to pick up a few boxes of trash and discovered it was a million dollars in cash someone dumped paranoid. All people chase money to the grave. However, pass up what they think looks like trash on the side of the road, speeding fast to notice the trash was actually a treasure and look at the fine details right in front of them. If you were consciously tapped into your environment and universal connected, you would have been aware to pick up the boxes off the side of the highway that can distract drivers, and you would've done preventions of accidents, possibly saving lives. With that little bit of energy of humanity and picking up the trash, cleaning the environment, conscious of the universe, you would've got rewarded back by the universe with a million dollars cash.

Develop your universal connection and awareness and your platform to push. Then connect with people and show them how to connect universal. Help structure to make them optimize sense of universal connection and awareness.

A lot of people always ask how to innovate. Innovation is introducing something new or a new way to do something that already exists to make better or simple versus complex. You need to think more practically, produce more new and different ways to think. Creativity, problem solving, or moving entities. Producing techniques to help you and process of judgement. Feel and intuition. How elegant is the truth. It's proprietor group to help you think and produce. Product and techniques help you think. Some people get going by dancing, moving in their rhythm flow. Music or whatever suits them best. Find things you are good at and what you love. The passion will be a sweet spot. Think about what you're interested in and enthusiastic about. That energy that pushes and motivates you to do it in bursts pumped eagerly. When you're motivated, your dopamine and reward system to push it to existence. You cannot write a novel if you're not naturally enthusiastic or energy into it. It will be harder, forced, and writer's block with half-finished or poor projects. Your heart has to be in it, not attached. You can train others in these innovation methods and insights.

Determine what the desired purpose is. Like if you want them to find their calling, start by engaging the audience in what you want. Set the tone. Then introduce an icebreaker action, like an exercise. Always demonstrate first before you ask someone to do. Introduce a concept or principle that will deliver on your promise. Create credibility. Drive your message, mission, movement home with a story or personal connections have the deepest impact. Have a clear transition from one message, movement, and push to the other. Do not confuse people, energy, or the universe with complexity or mixed signals. Some framework is to write 20 questions down to yourself and answer them honestly. Do this with a subject, cause, or push. See if your energy match, sincerity, and authenticity to the universe to where it will come spinning back around like the Earth or back down like the universal gravity. The best ideas, pushes, and messages solve the hardest problems with simple universal solutions and united universal energy.

The universal power of the people will be stronger than people in power. My universal connection and awareness to push out in the universe is to push the ILM movement and unite voices unmuted with BLM movement for people to listen, learn, and be aware to push for police and prison reform that affects both sides and Black families. Also push my universal connection energy to launch a petition to reform and a helluva change. I have a vision of a bill to break all injustice to end mass incarceration.

- Chapter 11 -

"ILM Movement"

Brandon Hullaby was an inner city youth going in-and-out of the prison system. He got set up with one of Phoenix's reverse sting operations, which was basically entrapment. He didn't actually do a crime, and the agents arrested him. He eventually went to trial and got found guilty, and the sentence was 35 years in the Federal BOP.

Hullaby and others were targeted by agents that go into these urban plagued neighborhoods to get minorities to do a multitude of criminal acts. Also to encourage these minorities to bring guns because it's a federal guideline mandatory minimum consecutive prison sentence if found guilty.

This was entrapment because they also induce, coerce, and provide minorities with guns, vehicles, and essential tools to railroad them. They basically pick you up and take you to get arrested.

This is something most people don't know even exists. They are doing Entrapment 101. In Arizona entrapment is basically nonexistent, whereas they don't look at it as law or acknowledge it, which is all that needs to be put under the microscope and seeing these agents going out of scope of the law and violating minorities' rights and freedom of choice, too.

They do not allow you to choose to disconnect, withdraw, or an official way out. We want to put an actual spotlight on these typical reverse sting operations that exist all across America: Florida, Arizona, California, Chicago, Houston, Nevada, etc.

This is what also leads to clogging the penal system with mass incarceration, too. That needs to stop and be reformed!

The Department of Justice, the U.S. Attorney all need to be held accountable, and systemic racism needs to be weaved out of these departments. Not just the police departments.

After Hullaby got sentenced to the 35 years, he was sent to USP Attwater, and he had made the choice to study law, educate and elevate himself.

He landed around some good mentors that taught him how to read, write, and speak law. He honed in and dedicated his time incarcerated and made it work for him wholeheartedly.

Mr. Brim, one of his mentors, held him accountable and told him if he wants to go home in 5 years to study. Hullaby stayed in the law library every day until he finally got blessed 2 whole years later to comprehend the language of the law and how it works to manifest his freedom of hard work and years of dedication.

His lawyer, Doug Passon, and his appeal lawyer, Dan Kaplen, also helped and never gave up on Brandon Hullaby.

His trial judge said in her opinion she did not want to give him 35 years and believed for this type of offense the punishment was harsh and he didn't deserve it. She stated she couldn't get him off the mandatory minimum.

Hullaby used the Begay and Johnson case law, where he won partial language in his case of the 924(c) which is the gun in the furtherance of a crime.

The judge granted Hullaby impartial of the language where she took off the 924(c) and resentenced him. Also rehabilitation that was part of the other side she used in her opinion to her discretion to take off the 25 years and gave Hullaby time served.

Therefore, because his time on the inside was used to self-reform, he completed programs, stayed focused, and showed the judge he was self-reformed and rehabilitated, including doing a documentary from the inside, where he was able to push that whole time up off him and walk free right up out of the courtroom once Judge Susan Bolton resentenced him.

Which had the whole lockdown society buzzing, and used as inspiration of the whole self-reform Incarcerated Lives Matter blueprint and foundation. Nelson Mandela said it first: We must self-educate.

When Hullaby got released, he started doing community-building. He also started his own businesses that served the urban communities, building personal and business credit, providing clothes, shelter, and feeding the homeless, plus financial classes. He life-coaches and mentors the community for betterment and mental health.

Hullaby also created Westwardhills Management Consultants and Desert Elite cleaning services, which he plans to go green. He continues to serve as a pillar of his community and influencer, the face of his community and Incarcerated Lives Matter, too.

Hullaby's aim in ILM is also to show the flip side of the coin on ILM and reverse sting operations of entrapment, the probation departments, and domestic violence, too.

He shed a spotlight on the probation department being petty with all these minor offenses. They violate people, taking them from their families, community, and workplaces, too. This causes clogs in the penal justice system and prisons that's also a key component to mass incarceration. The probation department is supposed to help the parolee or probationer to reintegrate and be successful in all reentry aspects. They need rehabilitation and not prisons. Again this is America's cure-all answer with punishment and prisons excessively.

Brandon Hullaby also wants to further shed a spotlight on domestic violence of the flip side of the coin on male victims, too, just like dirty deeds done cheap, where the man is the victim of domestic violence, too. The police, judge, and penal system don't have mercy on the masculinity of men that women exploit and use against them. It's been plenty of cases and circumstances where the man has gotten locked-up, sent to the grave or even a life sentence without no voice being a victim.

Hullaby plans to change all of that and the narrative, also giving a voice to the voiceless and being the face of the faceless that been hidden from society with miscarriages of justice.

There is such a thing as women victimizers that diligently seek men victims with ulterior motives. He also wants to free a lot of innocent men because he, too, can relate, personally being a victim of this same injustice being swept under the rug.

Brandon Hullaby and Hitachi Choparazzi that suffers from an illegal sentence error, both the face and the voice of ILM and cofounders of

ILM, plan to raise real awareness and push the ILM movement, doing a rally/march to the Lincoln Memorial in Washington, D.C. for ILM moms, dads, sisters, brothers, activists, women, community leaders, reform advocates, public, etc., to unite all. United we stand, forever we shall evolve.

After holding the ILM movement awareness rally in D.C., Brandon Hullaby and Hitachi Choparazzi, the face and the voice of ILM, plan to go to the White House to schedule a sitdown with V.P. Harris to talk real prison reform and finally addressing the 13th Amendment that keeps us all enslaved by the government since 1863 to end mass incarceration.

Epilogue

I would like to thank all you incarcerated, outside in the free world for your support, push, and awareness. BLM movement, reach out to us inside and tap into ILM movement. Contact me. Finally, all that I helped, healed, and taught how to reform, join the movement and passed down my same self-reform inside blueprint, mentality and lifestyle. I do this for y'all because you matter, too.

Everybody that enjoyed this message, my journey of life and transformation and book, share it, send to a loved one locked up or period. Share online, leave Amazon or Google book reviews, retweet, tag, post, and share on your social feed. Use the hashtag #ILM. I appreciate all the love and support.

I'd like to leave you all with a list of people I recommend you study, read their books, or listen to their messages and movements for your Bluetooth: Muhammad Ali, Nelson Mandela, Tupac Shakur, Malcolm X, Nipsey Hussle, Obama, T.D. Jakes, Jesse Jackson, Stanley 'Tookie' Williams, Martin Luther King, Jr., Bob Marley, Mother Teresa, Colin Kaepernick, Rev. Al Sharpton, Naeem Akhbar, M. Gandhi, and you will learn a lot of depth. This is a small amount of influential people. It's an archive list you can browse thru.

If you want to help fund ILM movement or my Chop-A-Style Publishing library for ILM, I need help to typeset, edit, cover design, ebook format, Audibles, ISBNs, STANs, etc. You can go to my funding page on my homepage. Also, to support the Billion Dollar Blueprint movement or get merch in your stores or city wholesale, hit my email. If you want to purchase music or ILM apparel for support, hit the home page, too, and tap in. All influencers and organizations that want to tap in, help with inside reform and prison reform, or fund me or us with donations, hit my email and trust agent.

Finally, if you want to book me for personal consultants, private tutors, speaking engagements, tattoos, training, personal development, sport events, ghost writer sessions, screenplay writer, motivational coaching, and innovation, once I'm finally free, email me. I love y'all.

Book Bonus Page

Finally, I would like to leave you all a book bonus to add value to self, community, and everyday lives, for ILM and BLM movement. Leave you all with some reform principles, code of conduct, and a poem I wrote for you to resonate. I love y'all. Be safe, be strong, be united and proactive. Blessings and lessons in life.

The 5 ILM and BLM Self-Reform Universal Principles of the Universal Blueprint

1. Sovereign Individuality

Awareness of one's self and your unique nature and role in family, society, and the universe. The conscious development of your gifts and skills. Refining your faculties and having personal discipline. Maintaining your physical, mental, and emotional health. The ability to evaluate, assess, study, understand, and have discernment. Defining yourself, proclaiming yourself, having a purpose. Being the seer and not the one seen. Perfect contentment and sense of worth in ALL circumstances.

2. Maat (Mot)

Harmonious system of differing parts worked into a whole. Justice and order, rhythm, coordination. Peace, common destiny, truth. Cooperative economics, collective work, and responsibility. Mutual aid and assistance, unity.

3. Persistent Dedication

Focus, steadfastness, ambition, and drive. Never complaining, relentlessness, never quitting. Full of energy and power, everlasting. Immortal, being reliable.

4. Creative Flexibility

Ability to adapt, bend without breaking. Resilience, overcome adversity and obstacles. Use what resources are available. The appropriate to any situation or dilemma. The ability to think, act, and make adjustments while in motion. Never being stagnant. Always open-minded. It's building blocks in knowledge. Remember, when you great, they hate; progress breeds success.

5. Courageous Self-Sacrifice

Actions without worrying about the benefits, pain or pleasure, reward or punishment. Having a sense of duty and service. Loving and protecting. Facing any challenge. Being true of your speech. Honesty.

ILM and BLM Code of Conduct

PHASE ONE:

1. No bragging, being the center of attention or drawing attention to one's self.

2. No complaining. No arguing and backbiting.

3. Always maintain an attitude and feelings of self-respect, self-love, and self-determination. Contentment (having enough and being satisfied). Not greedy.

4. Every day set aside at least one hour for meditation, thinking about your visions and your goals. Keep a journal and write your thoughts down. Have regular counseling sessions with your peers, mentors, or accountability groups.

5. Think about what you want to contribute to society. Write down your ideas and brainstorm a perpetual thought process. What is your worth?

6. At every opportunity, do for yourself! Do not ask for help or a handout until after you have tried to do it or figure it out yourself. Learn and/or teach yourself a side hustle or two. Write, program, arts and crafts, open an estore online, do Zoom fitness workout classes, etc.

7. Only cut down 2-3 hours of screen time, social media, or TV a day if you have either one or both. Try for no TV and little screen time as much as possible you can. Challenge yourself to use this digital

detox time to do something constructive and develop self or a new skillset.

8. Go to bed around 8:30 to 9 p.m. and get up by 4 to 5 a.m. No naps during the day unless you absolutely have to, and then no more than for a half an hour.

9. When you wake up every morning, no matter what, wash up, make your bed, and clean up. Personal hygiene and energy appearance. No excuses. Affirmations.

10. Work out at least 4x per week. Cardio, abs, push-ups, curls, leg routines, etc. Dedicate gym or exercise time religiously. Shape your body or it will shape you.

11. No cursing, no drugs, no smoking (or cut down to a discipline of one every hour or two). No sweets, added sugar, or salts. No fast food, junk food, or processed foods. Read for at least one hour a day, listen to an Audible, webinar, and write, probe, and structure for at least an hour per day.

12. No lying to impress others or cheating to get ahead, cutting corners. Put the time in, the long and hard way, not the fast speedy lane. Be present.

13. No vain talking or boasting. Only meaningful talking, building principles or necessary talk.

PHASE TWO

Start specializing as far as learning more about your chosen area of expertise and talent. Start thinking, acting, and speaking more in line with your position and role as a man/woman and leader in training.

You should be discussing our situation of oppression as a race with others. Thinking of ways to fight back. Talking about how to govern and protect our women, children, and communities. Forward thinking and problem solving. Write down blueprints. This is what men, women, and pillars of the community do! Define community involvement and write down ways you want to be involved. Start serving in some way. Define and study leadership and leaders. Start developing speaking and communication skills. Debate opposing viewpoints. Chair a meeting. Also adopt an authentic African original lifestyle and value systems like our all original African tribes, counsel, and practices. For example, Nguzo Saba and our Maat (pronounced MOT) principles. Create your own version that fits you!

OATH

I am a reflection of self, family, love, and my community for maximum building or each one teach and reach one.

I am not a slave, boy, or a nigga. I have risen out of bondage to my emotion, ignorance, selfishness, and materialism.

I am create free! I resist all forms of oppression, tyranny, and cruelty in the world.

As a freedom fighter activist, advocate, and member of ILM and BLM movements! I pledge my loyalty to the 5 ILM and BLM self-reform universal principles of sovereign individuality, maat, persistent dedication, creative flexibility, courageous self-sacrifice.

I swear upon life and truth to:

1. Embrace my purpose and responsibilities.

2. Seek self-knowledge and transformation to the grave.

3. Create ways to protect the inalienable rights of self and others.

4. Always serve the cause by building thru action!

Book Bonus Poem

Titled: Roses is Black & Violets are Red

When Roses is Black
And Violets are Red...
Is Black my People
And Red the Blood
Is Black my Power
And Red my Pain
Is Black my Shadow
And Red my Brain
Is Black my Rain
And Red my Chains
Is Black my Death
And Red my Breath...
Is Black COVID-19...
And Red the Vaccine...
—Hitachi Choparazzi

Their roses are red, ours is Black, power, and people. Their violets are blue, why is ours red from bloodshed? Our Black roses grow from the penitentiary, cemetery, and concrete. We say BLM and they chant Blue Lives Matter. Stop killing and locking us up! We not Black roses, we Black lives and life!

You'll see my efforts to change youth's and people's criminal mentality into a positive perspective. My additional bonus to add value to self, for your Bluetooth.

Do not break laws at all! The best recipe to beat the police, state, and feds is to avoid them, period. The best offense is defense. I know some situations involving the police you cannot avoid being victims of targeted racial profiling. However, you can defend yourself, take steps in your life began with consciousness, bring self-awareness, aware of your actions and surroundings. Most people blame each other, even laws. Some laws and government are farfetched and excessive. You are your worst enemy. People do what you allow them to do. You can start by avoiding crowds, parties, gangs, drugs, schemes, and most of all, following others. We need more leaders. Wrong company is bad results because you are your association and environment, which is proven in history time and time again. If your associates do things you don't, it will soon rub off on you, then have its effect on you sooner or later.

Remember, if you are in denial of anything, it is a problem right there. Watch the company you keep. Keep yourself busy with your tasks, goals, and dreams you're striving to complete. Have a spirituality about yourself. Practice religion, join a church, mosque, or temple, or maybe nondenominational. Our problem is everyone cares what the world's ways are and what people think of them. However, people hate criticism, will not listen to their parents, peers, or siblings about their flaws. Remember, people see in you what you do not see or want to acknowledge about yourself. Do not be afraid to ask people, what do you see that I need to work on? Or what do people say about me?

Lastly, my challenge to all youth and everyone is to put all of that same energy and time into something constructive, positive, and watch all the positive results to follow guaranteed. Do not shackle yourself and let them take your life to waste your life. I love y'all. Peace, blessings, positive energy vibes, and unity is all we need.

Article I

There is a flip side of the coin. And that flip side of Black Lives Matter is Incarcerated Lives Matter, all stemming from them same racial profiling and biased cops targeting the urban communities, young Black men, women, and juveniles. They become victims of systemic racism and part of the now 1.4 million incarcerated population, which clogs the system and end results of this now mass incarceration that we all need to push to fix because it's clear bias and broken. America is number one in data of the most incarcerated citizens of their country.

However, Afro-Americans make up only 17 percent of the United States population, but represents the most highest ethnic group incarcerated. Meaning young Black men, women, and juveniles is the majority population locked up in these human storage sheds, but the minority of the United States population.

That represents a huge black-and-white area, but an even bigger gray area. America punishment jail being a cure-all tool is not working. It should be rehabilitation and reentry reintegration versus punishment in excessive time. It's all now a billion-dollar for-profit business, especially with these private prisons, contracts, vendors, manufacturers, health providers specifically for prisons for-profit entity. These same entities, organizations, etc., have exclusive rights that are not regulated to the public interest or audited within a reasonable scope. It's even stock and IPOs with these same for-profit prison vendors, manufacturers, contractors, healthcare providers, and private prisons.

The United States 13th Constitutional Amendment states that slavery shall be abolished except for government slavery, meaning prisoners or imprisonment, which this United States Constitutional Amendment is just one of the focal points and aim to rewrite and change the Constitutional language that enslaves 1.4 million Americans. Incarcerated Lives Matter too, and this is only one merely long-term goal to achieve for us to end mass incarceration.

However, there are so many clearly flagrant issues of mass incarceration dealing with the penal system and systemic racism range from the judge's excessive sentencing, abuse of power. Also, prosecutor misconduct, fines, probation violations, petty crimes, and fees that imprison the poor people. The ineffectiveness of assistance of counsel pre-trial or during trial. Tainted and biased juror pools. Partial jury convictions, illegal sentences, conspiracy, and exaggerated drug laws that max Black people out. And the long list is too extensive to name each miscarriage of justice and injustice to the mass incarceration clog that plagues our institutions and community. It's clear evidence that is not equally yoked. And the fathers, leader, pillars, and mothers of the community are exiled.

This call for action is a call for attention and to put a direct spotlight on mass incarceration to build a platform of awareness with Incarcerated Lives Matter, too, and broaden the scope so we can all come together, the creatives, activist thinkers, community leaders, advocates, prison reform organizations, influencers, and unite to formulate effective solutions and everyone plays the part with their position they specialize in to enable us to break through to end mass incarceration in the systemic racism that plagues the criminal justice system. However, we must focus on the origin cause of arresting officers by targeting and harassing young Black men, women, and juveniles. Donald Trump and Republican for private prisons party donates.

If you believe Incarcerated Lives matter, too, and the flip side of the same coin as the crooked cops throwing Black men in their grave or a cage with malice and outstanding intention flagrant misconduct and targeted victims being hunted in the urban communities nationwide. This is a crisis and emergency. Even though they will not grant an emergency executive order to end mass incarceration due to monetizing and human trafficking business, they will counter-claim public safety risk.

Article II

Question...Do you believe Incarcerated Lives Matter, too?

Metaphor: You can hear the dead crying out from the grave, but you cannot hear the echoes of the slaves in the cage?

This was an example metaphor I used in my book I wrote from within the toxic walls of lockdown society titled Incarcerated Lives Matter Movement: The Hitachi Choparazzi Blueprint as a subtitle.

I wrote this ILM book to spread awareness, the ILM movement, the self-reform blueprint for ILM, and the main premise, unity. For BLM and ILM to unite both movements and push as a whole effectively. I believe you cannot be fully woke out there until you're aware and conscious about what's going on inside here. Also about the problematic mass incarceration of 1.4 million people due to the same systemic racism cops' malicious and targeted arrest and misconduct to an already broken system. However, if you truly want to restructure, reform, or abolish something, you have to know how it works and the heart of it. Therefore, you cannot truly understand the ongoing problematic issues of mass incarceration fully until you tap in. By you tapping into Incarcerated Lives Matter and lockdown society, you will see all the important scope of injustices in your own city and state. The aim is for us incarcerated to come together as lockdown society under one huge umbrella as Incarcerated Lives Matter to adopt this movement, format, and reform blueprint to push as a whole and have the outside people and community to back us up and be our voice and frontline pushers, too, that we can problem solve and simplify effective solutions together to end mass incarceration. They may silence us individually being incarcerated with no voice. This is why I used my writing and creating an ILM book as a tool for others and a megaphone. Whereas, they cannot silence us all, lockdown society as a whole united voice and demand from every state, federal, and county facility raising every voice for the same push and change.

Incarcerated Lives Matter will be one united movement and push for prison reform and to end mass incarceration. Also one platform for all to state their injustice, awareness, voice be heard, and to connect with the outside community and loved ones. Including projects, legal help, funding, institutional aid, cruel and unusual punishment/conditions, reentry resources, mental health, housing, employment, job skill training, and all incarcerated congruences. To cast one big web of net as lockdown society state-to-state ILM chapters with bros and sisters of progress and leadership skills inside and outside.

I started and co-founded this movement 3 years ago. However, more recently after seeing George Floyd savagely choked out for almost 9 whole minutes made me have a flashback reaction from the OPD choking me out till I blacked out all the way sparked an unrested rage in me stemming from the brutality and scars I sustained due to being profiled and a targeted victim, which sparked me to ignite a fuel to write this book never formulated or told from a real life experience form living it and being a victim to it. Both sides of the flipped coin, whether heads or tails, meaning in the grave or a cage, police brutality and misconduct or their trumped-up charges and vindictive arrests that lack probable cause.

For years as a Black man from NYC, Midwest, down South, eventually to the West Coast, I lived and experienced it all. Only difference is some states worse than others. However, it's all the same systemic racism and being targeted. Makes you feel like you don't matter. Especially after they throw you in a cage. You feel nonexistent, like you lost your right at life to live, educate, or have an opinion. This being oblivious to the world in a real-life human storage facility out of sight, out of mind, is merely an understatement. The ILM book also goes further in depth about this matter issue throughout the whole entire book.

However, I could not read or write until I got older and had a typical hood story stemming from the projects, no father or structure, instead the wrong influences, choices, and environment led to the streets gripping me by the throat. From gangs, selling drugs, pimpin, you name it, I lived it. Being incarcerated, going thru it to grow thru it and finding self, meditating, and being conscious while reading helped me to tap into my gifts, mind, and universe. It helped me to do a 180 straight turnaround and use the prison as my platform by extracting value out of it by reversing my time, making it work for me, not against me. Educating myself, learning new and different skillsets, and reading everything for betterment and personal development to assist me in my transition. All led up to me doing a self-reform, which the same successful structure I used can be duplicated and implemented by anyone free or incarcerated.

This is the same ILM Hitachi Choparazzi Blueprint in the subtitle I am referring to as well. Along with prison reform, police reform, COVID-19 inside lockdown society, the universal push and my solutions. Also I cannot forget to mention the chapter solely dedicated to the subject line of influencers, organizations, advocates, etc., all tap in and give these Black men, women, and juveniles a second chance. Help them, employ them, give them contracts, resources, placements, funding, artist deals, etc. It's hidden jewels behind these fences and walls you cannot see, with a lot of full promising potential. The state and feds use them as merely cheap laborers to build as they did our ancestors. One of my pet peeves is when people say, "That's a great idea, but wait till you get out." No! Utilize time now!

About Author

Hitachi Choparazzi is a New York City native, by the way of Omaha, who is currently incarcerated in level 5 solitary confinement in Florence, SMU-Eyman Complex, serving an illegal sentence awaiting on Supreme Court Appeal to correct his sentence with time served. The error forces him to serve 2 years extra.

He is an entrepreneur, tattoo artist turned author. Also the sole owner of Chop-a-Style Publishing and Productions, and the owner of Chatmon Sr. Literary Agency. He has written over 20 books and including scripts to pitch to Netflix. All this while he was incarcerated to start his reform act.

Founder and CEO of Billion-Dollar Blueprint and the BDB movement/ youth movement, an innovator entrepreneurship where he believes everyone has their own blueprint, like everyone has their own unique thumbprint. Based on 3 core principles—Education, Elevation, and

Innovation—which he teaches the youth and people how to format and discovery key. BillionDollarBlueprintmerch.com

The face of lockdown society movement along with the voice of lockdown society movement. IncarceratedLivesMovement.com #ILM #BDB

"I do this for y'all. I love y'all, rep y'all, and believe in y'all! I won't stop giving y'all all the raw stories as God bless them in my head. I have a hundred of them up there. Anybody that has a hot hand, send me samples or any comments, suggestions to my FB, IG Hitachi Choparazzi or email: orders@chopastylepublishingllc.com Chop-A-Style Publishing LLC and Productions. TeflonLuv!"

Hitachi Choparazzi prides himself on having his own signature Chop-a-Style where he freestyles all his books. They all rhyme with innovation and original storylines. He writes prequels, sequels, trilogies, and more. Does it for the people who love to read and for all those incarcerated in state, federal B.O.P., county, and women's facilities. FB,IG,Tiktok, Twitter, YouTube-Hitachi Choparazzi

Emails: Hitachichoparazziauthor@gmail.com Billiondollarblueprintmerch.com

Chop-A-Style Publishing and Productions LLC

Other Books and Scripts by the Author

Non-Fiction

- How to Rap; The Elementary Teaching of Hip-Hop

- How To Tattoo & Start-Up Business

- How To Digital Detox

- How To Start-Up a Food Truck Business

- How To Stop School and Mass Shootings: Dear Parents

- Incarcerated Lives Matter: The Hitachi Choparazzi Blueprint

- How to Love

- The Switch: A Social Awareness Self-Help

- Nipsey Hussle Lockdown Society Dedication–Tribute

- If Trayvon Martin Could Talk; Injustice

Fiction

- The Eagle and Weasel (1-5 series kids' book)

- She Go! (urban novel)

- Reality Show 3D-HD (urban novel)

- Hot Thots (urban novel)

- Liqz (urban novel)

- Paranormal Whisper (horror novel)

- Pimp of Da Ratchets (urban novel)

- Pimp of Da Ratchets II Vegas (urban novel)

- Pimp of Da Ratchets 3 Orange is Da New Pimp (urban novel)

- Hitachi (urban novel)

- Penitentiary Pimp (urban novel)

- Weasel Society (urban novel)

- The Big Pep and Plucker Story-She Go! Prequel (urban novel)

Screenplays/Scripts

- Top Notch

- Hot Thots

- Pimp of Da Ratchets

- Weasel Society

- Million Dollar Games–A Secret Society

- The Eagle and Weasel (animation)

Available at Barnes and Noble and Amazon

Welcome to the exclusive lives of 4 extremely hot THOTs. This book will show you how to spot a THOT. From THOT tops to THOT flops, all the way to THOT Snaps and claps.

This book is the first-ever with a double twisted love triangle. Watch as Chicago, LA, ATL, and Seattle THOTs entwine at Coachella.

Some on fleek and some looking cheap, but they all cheat! They all commit aTHOTery with their THOTery acts, shameless.

Raunchy, with steaming hot sex scenes to sex swings. From wild threesome ménages, and twerking, to bare-it-all raw. Too hot! THOT gum pop...

This page-turner is an eye-opener to the very end, with a bombshell-dropping, shocking ending. The secret life of THOTs

Available at Barnes and Noble and Amazon

Billion Dollar Blueprint is a movement we challenge and inspire you to find your individual blueprint. Our mantra is "We believe everyone has their own blueprint like everyone has their own thumbprint". With these three core principles

Education

Elevation

Innovation

Hitachi Choparazzi is the founder and CEO. Orders available to support incarcerated businesses.

Orders available at: billiondollarblueprintmerch.com